To Maria

You true desires
are manifesting now!.

Blessings to you.

— Victor Lavalle-Cor

MANIFESTING YOUR DESIRES

How To Apply Timeless Spiritual Truths To Achieve Fulfillment

A Self-Study Course

Victoria Loveland-Coen, RScP

MANIFESTING YOUR DESIRES

How To Apply Timeless Spiritual Truths To Achieve Fulfillment

A Self-Study Course

by

Victoria Loveland-Coen

Illustrations by:
Ricardo Abrines

Additional Illustrations by:
Nancy Ramirez

Cover Art by:
David Leytus

Published by:
SELF-MASTERY PRESS
P.O. Box 57272
Sherman Oaks, CA 91413

Copyright 1995, 1998 by Victoria Loveland-Coen
First printing: 1995
Second printing: 1998 completely revised and expanded
ISBN # 0-9644765-0-9

The manifestation of this book was greatly assisted by the love and support of a few special individuals.

An abundance of thanks goes to:

My husband, Dana Coen, who gave me the gift of time and placed before me the goal of excellence. My practitioner, Angela Coxton, for her powerful prayers for my consciousness and for this project.
My dear friend Rhonda Britten who's support and encouragement was unwavering. My friend Ricardo Abrines for the gift of his lovely illustrations. Shawn Kelly for the stunning book cover. Gary Krakower for guiding me through an unfamiliar computer program.
The continuing inspiration I receive from my spiritual community, Agape International Center of Truth.
And to my mother, Olive T. Loveland whose very life will always remain an inspiration to me.

CONTENTS

Preface: i

Chapter One: Desires   1

Chapter Two: Nature of Reality   19

Chapter Three: Who Are We?   33

Chapter Four: Our Creative Nature   43

Chapter Five: Authentic Self & False Self   57

Chapter Six: Core Beliefs   75

Chapter Seven: The Law of Attraction   97

Chapter Eight: The Power of Forgiveness   117

Chapter Nine: The Power of Meditation   131

Chapter Ten: Treatment   142

Chapter Eleven: Inspired Action   167

Chapter Twelve: Summary   175

Appendix / Resourse Guide   181

Congratulations! By acknowledging that your heart contains desires which you suspect can be fulfilled, you have taken the first step toward accomplishing that goal. Because you have purchased this self-study course to learn the techniques for achieving such goals, you have taken the second step. So you see, you are well on your way. In fact, the fulfillment of your true desires is even now in process!

This book is a culmination of twenty-five years of study, research and direct experience. It began when I was sixteen, on the island of Coronado off the coast of San Diego. My mother and I were at the beautiful home of fellow "Truth seekers" and were being initiated, one at a time, into Transcendental Meditation. This experience opened wide my consciousness to an entirely new perspective on life. But, it was only the beginning.

Being a child of the sixties, I instinctively knew to question the assumptions of the status quo. From my perspective, established institutions, religious constructs and modes of thinking didn't seem to be working for most. My mind was opening to the possibility that there was another reality, a power of love, and a way of living, of which I was beginning to catch but a glimpse. My thirst for more knowledge was unquenchable.

Thus began my endless search for Truth, which lead me to many insightful books, including: The Science of Mind, Autobiography of a Yogi, A Course in Miracles, Be Here Now, The Teaching of the Masters of the Far East, Scientific Christian Mental Practices, The Tao of Physics, Being a Christ, Spiritual Economics and many others. I investigated the books and teachings of Emerson, Thomas Troward, Norman Vincent Peale, Catherine Ponder, John Randolph Price, Joel Goldsmith, Dr. Wayne Dyer, and more recently, Deepak Chopra, Marianne Williamson and Reverend Dr. Michael Beckwith. I have studied The Teaching of the Inner Christ, Eastern religions, Unity, Yoga, Parapsychology, Mysticism, Mental Science and Religious Science among others.

Throughout my journey the one discipline which has remained constant is meditation. While the method I practice now is my own discipline and no longer formally TM, meditation remains a vital part of my ongoing spiritual awakening. You will learn more about why meditation is so essential, and be given step-by-step instructions for your own experience of this transformational process in chapter nine.

In the last several years my course of study has centered around The

Science of Mind where I trained to become a licensed Religious Science Practitioner. ("RScP" is the professional designation.) A Religious Science Practitioner is essentially a professional spiritual counselor who utilizes the techniques of spiritual mind treatment to promote healing for their clients.

There are universal truths in every religion and philosophy, and I have drawn from as many as speak to me. The term God is used throughout this book and is interchangeable with the terms Universe, Spirit, Source and Universal Intelligence among others. When I refer to God, it is not the archaic idea of God as an old man with a beard sitting on a cloud, looking over our shoulder to check if we're being good or not, if we're deserving or not. It has never made sense to me how a God who is the essence of Love could withhold blessings to any one of It's children. The idea of God as judgmental and malicious, who's kinder to some and harsher to others is a God created in *our own* image. Perhaps because that's the way *we* are and it's difficult to imagine a God who loves everyone equally, and desires only the highest good for all. But this is, in fact, the truth. As you will learn, the Universe cannot possibly play favorites. Rather than thinking of God as an entity — a noun — it might be helpful to think of God as a verb – a Power of Love, or a Principle of limitless good.

This "self-study course" does more than present spiritual or metaphysical theory, it gives you a method for making this theory functional in your life. The techniques you will learn are those I have used successfully myself, with my clients on an individual basis, and with groups in workshops. Indeed you will learn how to apply spiritual principle to achieve fulfillment in any area of your life.

Following are tips on achieving success with this material:

- Read the book one chapter at a time — in sequence. For a deep and comprehensive understanding, do not skip chapters. Individual concepts are revealed at specific times by design.

- Do *all* the suggested exercises within each chapter. Also, feel free to write down your thoughts in the margins, or on any of the blank pages. This is a *workbook*.

- There is an audiocassette available from Self-Mastery Press, read by the author, which contains most of the exercises as well as the guided meditation. This may provide a more complete experience of the processes and exercises — particularly those which are done with eyes closed. See the back page of this book to order.

- Take your time with the material. Some of the concepts within are foreign to our usual way of understanding how the world works. A slow and easy pace will help you digest the ideas thoroughly.

We at Self-Mastery Press are confident you will have success with this self-study course and are interested in hearing about your progress. So, please write and share your stories, or thoughts with us.

Along with the book, we are sending our love and a special blessing:

May your mind be open, your understanding deep,
and may you experience the fulfillment
of all your heart's desires!

C HAPTER ONE

DESIRES

*"I am the immeasurable potential of what was, is and
will be and my desires are like seeds left in the ground.
They wait for the right season and then spontaneously
manifest into beautiful flowers and might trees,
into enchanted gardens and majestic forests."*
—Rig Veda

Desire frequently gets a bad rap in our society. It's as if there is a tacit agreement among us not to discuss our desires openly, or seriously. Hence, many of us have *secret* desires. We don't share them with others and we don't give them much room in our own consciousness. Perhaps we think it's somehow selfish to want too much for ourselves; as if we would be taking something away from others if we had the fulfillment of our dreams.

Or, we dismiss our heart's desires with a "It would be nice, but that'll never happen" attitude. Why waste our time dreaming if our desires are unobtainable anyway? After all, it's not normal to have *everything* we desire. In fact, most of us don't know many people who have fulfilling, successful careers doing what they love, *and* have a loving relationship with the spouse of their dreams, *and* have an abundance of prosperity, *and* have perfect health and ageless beauty. We may have *read* about some star in People Magazine who is living the life of their dreams. However, we rationalize that they're "special" or just "very lucky." We may even be envious of their lives. If so, we are subconsciously telling ourselves that we could never have such luck, because we're different than them. We're saying subliminally: "Who am I to have the fulfillment of my heart's desires? I'm not lucky or special. Besides, they could lose everything they had, and then where would they be? Ruined. At least I've learned to tolerate the mild stream of misery in my life."

We think that not having our dreams fulfilled is natural. "That's life" we say — and *believe*. So, we rationalize our desires away. But, by doing so, we're pushing away any possible fulfillment of those desires and embracing life's cruel fate. When we negate our heart's desires we lose our passion for living, and oftentimes we become bitter. Repressing our dreams arrests our growth as individuals and life becomes mundane and dry. Ironically, we feel we're somehow more "mature" when we learn to tolerate disappointment and unfulfillment. In fact, some of us even wear it like a badge of honor.

The idea that unfulfillment is normal is simply a perception. Perceptions do not necessarily have anything to do with truth. Where do these perception originate? Well, many of us were brought up by parents who warned us not to "get our hopes up." "Now little Billy (or Jimmy or Vicki, etc.) you are going to have to realize that you can't have everything you want," they warned us. "You're going to have to get used to the "real" world where there are many disappointments. That's just the way thing are, dear." Most of us have been programmed to believe at least some variation on this theme. We're told that dreams only come true in fairy tales and Disney movies — the stuff of childhood fantasy, and that it's *unrealistic* to expect dreams to come true in the grown up world. This perception of the how the "real" world works gets passed down generation after generation.

> "To a large degree, reality is whatever the people who are around at the time agree to."
>
> —*Milton H. Miller*

Of course, our parents were well-meaning. They were trying to spare us from a life of pain and disappointment. To one degree or another, pain and disappointment have been their experience. In order to survive, they learned to tolerate frustration, unhappiness and unfulfilled dreams. This is our role model. This is what we learned was normal. And so, we either learn not to pay attention to our dreams and desires, as they have nothing to do with the "real" world, *or* we get caught in the wishing and hoping stage. Some of us become like Walter Mitty, daydreaming of a more magnificent life, *but deep down, believing it's not possible for u*s.

This is the game *I* played. I always dreamed of being a famous actress. I would fantasize about how my life would be when I became successful and admired for my talent. It was a constant daydream for years. Then, later on, because I wanted it so badly, and because I was daring and rebellious, I began to take my daydreams a step further — I risked the process of making the dream a reality. So, I did all the things one needs to do to launch an acting career. I studied with the recommended acting teachers, put my "headshots" and resume together, did showcases, acquired an agent and went to all the auditions. I worked very hard to make my dream come true. I did, in fact, have some initial success. Soon, however, a deep feeling of unworthiness began to emerge.

Because of the beliefs I had accepted at an early age, I never really felt like I *deserved* to have my dreams fulfilled. This consciousness served to sabotage my budding career and held it in stasis from then on. I spent the next eight years wishing, hoping and dreaming, but getting nowhere. I was completely unaware of the self-sabotaging mechanism that was operating in my life. I lived in envy of those "special" or "lucky" *successful* actors who always seemed to be

4

in the right place at the right time, unaware that I was telling my creative mind I could never have such luck.

Ultimately, this experience became the catalyst that led me to a deep exploration of how consciousness shapes our reality. Later in this book you'll learn how this self-sabotaging mechanism works and, more importantly, how to free yourself of its tyranny.

For now, perhaps you have a deep desire to have a fulfilling, successful and joyous life which is currently only in a dream state. Perhaps you're beginning to question those old self-defeating concepts. Although you would never tell anyone, maybe there's something within you that is secretly convinced that those childhood fairy-tales might actually be true after all. Perhaps you suspect there is indeed a key to manifesting your desires — a secret those "lucky" people have learned, but no one's told *you* yet. Possibly you already inwardly sense what this secret is and you only need confirmation. Perhaps it is this spirit which prompted you to buy this book. You may even be so bold as to suspect that you were created for a more magnificent life and that it is indeed within your reach. If so, you are right. You were, and it is!

A Natural Process

Far from being a secret, fulfillment of true desire is a natural process, it is how the universe operates. The universe is constantly expanding — there are new forms of life being created and expressed every day. Galaxies are formed, flowers bloom, trees bear fruit and babies are born. It is the nature of the Universe to come to fruition. We take it for granted.

Consider a rose bush. It doesn't need to struggle to create blossoms. It doesn't worry that it won't bloom. It doesn't question whether it's worthy of such beauty. It doesn't feel it's lucky. It just blooms. The essential nature of the rose bush is to express its glory and magnificence. This is the fulfillment of its true desire. True desires are intended to be fulfilled!

What's truly remarkable is that the seed of a rose contains all the elements necessary to become a rose bush resplendent with beautiful blossoms. It only needs the nurturing of soil and water. The rose seed is the rose bush in potentiality. Our desires are similar to the rose seed, because *inherent in having a desire, is everything necessary for its fulfillment.* It only needs a little nurturing.

Your desires are a potentiality waiting for your permission
to be released into actuality.

Desire is, in fact, the first step in the manifestation process. We would
have never accomplished anything in life if we lacked desire. We would never
have planted crops, built houses, created cities, founded or attended schools,
written books, sewed clothes, cut our hair or even taken a bath without first
desiring something that was not in existence at that moment. Desire is the start-
ing point for everything. It is essential to growth and evolution.

Let me clarify that I'm speaking about your *heart's desires* here, not passing
fancies or physical urges. Your true desires are those which have been tugging on
your heart for some time. It is the yearning, deep within you, to expand into a
greater expression and enjoy a more glorious, love-filled, abundant, creative and
fulfilling life. In fact, we could define true desire as an invitation from your inner
wisdom to express your potential — to be more than you thought you ever could
be.

So, what are your heart's desires? Could it be a fulfilling career; a youth-
ful and healthy body; finding your "soul-mate;" living in a beautiful and harmonious environment; a new business or completion of a cherished project; unshak-
able peace of mind; boundless abundance; or the expression of some latent talent? Maybe it's all of the above. Maybe your true desires have yet to identified.
You only know that you desire something greater than your current experience.
Whatever your dream may be it is meant for you to have and experience. As long
as your desires do no harm to yourself or anyone else, they are your inner self
urging you forward — urging you into the magnificent life you were meant to
live!

We want to welcome our heart's desires and encourage them to emerge
from the dream-state and express in reality — not *wishing*, not *dreaming*, but
consciously inviting our desires to naturally blossom from their seed. When we
consciously accept this natural blossoming process, we are taking the first step in
the manifestation process.

Free your mind forever from the belief that the Universe demands sacri-
fice or that God is more pleased with a person who can tolerate a life of poverty

or struggle. Nothing could be further from the truth! As one who had great understanding said: *"Let the Lord be magnified which hath pleasure in the prosperity of his servant"* (Psalms 35:27). Indeed, the Universe is more completely expressed through greater experiences of joy, peace and prosperity!

A New Beginning

Are you tired of tolerating a life that is less than fulfilling? Are you fed up with unhappiness, loneliness, ill health, repeated failure or mere survival? If so, good! As the saying goes, "If you keep doing the same things, in the same way, you'll keep getting the same results." This is a new moment; the time has arrived for transformation! The blessing of negative experience is that, if you allow it, it can act as a catalyst to open your heart and mind to a life far greater than you could have imagined. It is from darkness that much of life is birthed. The time is now to let go of limiting experiences and to begin accepting a fuller, richer, more rewarding journey through life. With the tools you will learn in this manual, your experience will act as a springboard out of misery and into peace, joy and the manifestation of your true desires.

Now, this path you are about to embark upon — this way of thinking — may seem a bit strange, if not completely foreign at first. However, choosing the path of independent thinking will make all the difference in your life. Remember what Robert Frost told us in *The Road Not Taken?*

> Two roads diverged in a wood, and I—
> I took the one less traveled by,
> And that has made all the difference.

On the road *most* traveled there is no choice — there is only reaction. Those on it soak up information they receive from the mass consensus — the media: television, radio, magazines, newspapers, or respected leaders, and react by robotically repeating those ideas that fit their personal prejudices. There is no choice as to what to think, what to feel, or what to believe. *True choice* can only be generated from a wisdom, and trust, found deep within. Most simply accept the limitations taught to them from outside sources, without ever investigating whether or not it's true. The opinion that "it can't be done" is enough to stop eighty-five percent of the population. Most allow the media, statistics or the assumptions of others to choose for them. Ten percent will take their goals a step further and won't give up until they hear from several "experts" that "it can't be done." It's that rare five percent that ignores anyone who says they can not have the fulfillment of their true desires. These individuals will not allow anyone, even "the experts," to tell them it can't be done. To think independently from the general agreement of society takes courage — or rather, an inner conviction. Therefore this road is, by definition, the one less traveled.

What would happen if we opened our minds to accept a new perspective of how life works? Would we be lost if we began to deconstruct our time-honored constructs? Or, would we be taking the first step toward ultimate freedom? Actually, the most freeing thing we can do is to begin questioning accepted limitations.

In the mid 19th Century, an Englishman by the name of Thomas Troward who was passionate about questioning accepted beliefs, began conducting scientific research on the power of thought. He had this to say about the value of discovering "truth," independent of preconceived assumptions:

> "The old limited mode of thought has imperceptibly slipped away, and we discover that we have stepped out into a new order of things where all is liberty and life. This is the work of an enlightened intelligence resulting from persistent determination to discover what truth really is irrespective of any preconceived notions from whatever source derived, the determination to think honestly for ourselves instead of endeavouring to get our thinking done for us."

The first step on the path of manifesting desires is to begin listening to that "still, small voice" within you. It's there right now, whispering to you about the wonderful life you deserve, the wonderful life it wants you to have. Everyone has this inner voice. This is your internal wisdom that is right now nudging you to move forward into a greater expression of life. Generally, if something "feels right in your gut," it's your inner voice speaking. The more you are aware of this voice, the stronger it will become.

Specific steps to nurture this inner guidance will be revealed in Chapter

Ten. For now, just know that the easiest way to tune into this voice is to become as quiet as you can. It will speak to you through your heart, nudging you gently at first, and if you follow its wisdom, *the Universe will conspire to support you.* If you ignore it, it will nudge you again. If you ignore it again, it will nudge you even more strongly. If we continuously ignore our inner wisdom and refuse to move forward, the Universe may need to give us a "push." Sometimes being pushed to the edge is the only way we get the message.

This "push" can be experienced in various ways. For example: you may become miserable at your job, or may even be terminated. You may become intolerably frustrated with your partner; perhaps he or she might even leave you. You may become sick, forcing your body to remain still long enough so that your mind may do some re-evaluating and soul searching.

If you are meant to move forward into a greater life, *you will do so sooner or later,* one way or the other. Why not take the subtle hints and do it without the pain! As Rev. Michael Beckwith of the Agape Center for Truth says: *"Allow yourself to be pulled by your vision, rather than being pushed by the pain."*

One of the ways to accomplish this is to focus on what you *do* want rather than what you *don't* want and allow the inspiration from that vision to gently pull you to it. This may sound simplistic, but it's not easy — it takes practice. We human beings seem to have an aptitude for focusing on what we *don't* have and what's *not* right. Some of us become comfortable with the pain of unfulfillment — like it were an old tattered sweater. It looks awful, but it's comfortable. So comfortable that, after a while we don't notice how bedraggled it is.

We also love to share our pain with others. Some take every opportunity they can find to talk of their misery. "No one loves me, I have no career, the government has taken all my money, my back is killing me, I was never given love as a child — but I'll be okay. I'm fine, really." And, those who love to share their tales of woe always find others who will support their staying small. "Life's been so tough for you," they say and you agree, multiplying the "victim consciousness" and increasing feelings of powerlessness.

Being Pulled By Your Vision

The exercises at the end of this chapter are designed to explore your vision — what your heart desires — and to pull it into focus. The more you work with it, the more it will appear in the forefront of your consciousness and the more you will be led to know exactly what to do to facilitate its appearance in your life. You will experience the life you desire first in your vision, for it is there that you plant and nurture the seed which will begin to open, allowing the sprout of creation to shoot forth into life.

All great athletes know the importance of holding, in their mind's eye, the accomplishment of their dream. For example, Bruce Jenner who broke the world's record in the decathlon event winning the Olympic gold medal in 1976, credits his success to an unwavering intention to win, coupled with his practice of mentally picturing the outcome.

Jim Carrey explained in a Barbara Walters' interview that, night after night, he would stand on a hillside overlooking the Los Angeles basin and visualize producers offering him $10 million to star in their picture. And, *he would stay there until he believed it.* This was quite a vision, considering he was barely scraping by at the time. Don't you think everyone, including those producers, told him he was dreaming, that it was an impossible goal? You bet! Did he listen to them? No — he held steadfast to his dream and is now paid $10 million to star in a film.

Did Bruce Jenner listen to the those who tried to warn this self-described "just-above-average" kid that it was physically impossible for him? Did he listen to those who wanted to spare him the pain of disappointment? No — both Jenner and Carrey had a true desire, a clear vision *and* the courage of their inner conviction.

> "Reach beyond your grasp. Your goals should be grand enough to get the best of you."
>
> — *Teilhard de Chardin*

Now, this should in no way imply that we cannot enjoy our lives until we reach our goals. Indeed we must! Otherwise, like horses with blinders, we'll focus only on the finish line. We should always honor the learning process and smell the roses along our path, enjoying each day to the fullest, recognizing and praising our growth — even if it "looks messy" at present. An "attitude of gratitude" expands the blessings we already have, and opens the portals for more good to pour into our lives. We want to enjoy each moment as is, confidently moving in the direction of our goals. Our aim is to develop and nurture our highest vision for our lives, while trusting that each experience (no matter how it appears) is the perfect unfoldment of that vision. We want to develop the trust that we are being guided everyday — every step of the way — into fuller and greater expressions of our potential.

> "When you come to the edge of the light you know, and you are about to step off into the darkness of the unknown, faith is knowing one of two things will happen. There will be solid ground for you to stand on...or you will be taught to fly!"
>
> *—Anonymous Sage*

Analogy:

In the film, *Indiana Jones and the Last Crusade*, Indiana races to save his father's life but finds himself staring at an abyss at the end of a tunnel. On the far side of the abyss is an opening, but it is clearly too far to leap across. Behind him, his adversaries draw close. Previously, an inscription written on an ancient tablet told him to "step from the head of the lion." Below him, carved into the stone is,

11

indeed, the head of a lion. However, according to what he sees, there is nothing to step out on. Because of his love for his father, he embraces his faith and steps out onto...a bridge, a bridge that was camouflaged so that it looked invisible. When the villains arrive at the tunnel, they lack the "vision" to see the bridge and are halted in their pursuit.

When you learn to trust the highest vision for your life and begin to move in that direction, you will be shown exactly where to step and how to leap over any seeming obstacle.

Get Specific

It's vital that we be as specific as possible regarding our desires. A clearly defined *intention* to which we give our *attention* becomes a magnet that attracts whatever is needed to bring it to fruition. A clearly defined intention also keeps us focused and committed to doing whatever is necessary on our part to make it a reality. As Mary Manin Morrissey tell us in her book, *Building Your Field of Dreams:*

> "You must be willing to take responsibility for your wishes and desires if you want to make them real. If you merely wish for a greater life, but do not specifically channel your energies into charting that future, the life force moving through you has no definite direction. When you hold an intention, you direct energy. If you do not consciously intend your dream to become reality, you unconsciously intend that something else will take form. Your very nature directs energy. The greatest control you have in your life is the power to direct the thoughts that help your dream take form."

In one of Lili Tomlin's humorous monologues, she remarked (in character) "I always wanted to be somebody, I realize now, I should have been more specific."

In the following exercise you will define your true desires thereby igniting the spark which will soon become a glowing flame.

EXERCISE: ***Discovering, Clarifying and Defining Your Desires***

This is a "visioning" exercise which is a bit different than visualization. In visualization, you have a specific goal in mind. Your attention is then focused on the goal for the purpose of directing the energy to bring it about. Visualization is an effective tool to use for specific purposes, but it can be limiting.

The visioning will take you a bit deeper. Visioning opens the door to unacknowledged blessings which may be simply waiting for your recognition. You may not yet know the full desires of your heart, but your inner wisdom does. Visioning connects you with the source of your inner wisdom. It works as you open your mind to see its view of you as a magnificent, successful, joyous, glorious and fulfilled being, here on this earth, at this particular time, for a specific purpose. Once you have the vision, you will establish it as your intention which will initiate the process of manifestation. Your vision will grow and expand over time, but will always serve as a source of support and inspiration throughout your life.

🕒 Give yourself 20 to 30 minutes of uninterrupted time to complete this exercise.

Read over the following instructions twice, then close your eyes and begin. You may also have someone read the exercise to you while you do it.

Close your eyes. Take a deep breath in, and then out. Again, breathe in stillness and breathe out the concerns of the day. Take one more deep breath of peace in and let it out. Let go of all concerns and allow your mind to become as quiet as possible. Tell your conscious thoughts that you'll get back to them later. Let your mind fall into the "spaces between your thoughts." This is where your "still, small voice" resides; it is your inner wisdom. It has been waiting patiently for you to connect with it. You are now giving it permission to whisper to you. What it is telling you? Your inner wisdom has a grand vision of life for you. Open your mind to see what that may look like. Look at the *overall* picture. Be sure not to censor yourself with thoughts such as "Well, I'm too old for that," or "I'll never have the money for that," or "The opportunities have passed me by," etc. Put these limiting voices aside for now and concentrate on what makes your heart sing.

What is your inner wisdom's vision for your life? Take another deep breath and open your heart even more. What is it telling you? You may hear a voice, see an image, or get a feeling. Try to capture a sense of this envisioned life as a present reality. Imagine it. See it. Feel it. What are you doing? Are you excited to get up every morning and go to a job you love? Are you taking relaxing, romantic vacations? Where? Are people respecting and admiring you? Are you surrounded by friends and family members who love and support you? Do you have the relationship of your dreams? What does that look like? Are you loving and supportive of others? Do you have health and plenty of vitality to enjoy life to the fullest? Do you have an abundance of money to buy beautiful things that add joy to your life? Are you confident, poised and fearless? Are you contributing some great talent or gift to the world? What is your unique expression, and how are you expressing it? Does what you do affect the lives of others? If so, in what way?

Stay with this vision for a while and let yourself enjoy it! Then when you feel complete about it, open your eyes, pick up a pen or pencil and use the space below to write it down. Be sure to state it in the present. For example: "*I am* enjoying waking up in my beautiful new home and going to my fulfilling job where *I am* surrounded by harmonious and supportive people," etc. Remember this does not have to be the final version. It can be amended and updated at any time.

i am happy to be recovering from my numerous surgeries and to have another chance at life. i love my family and enjoy my relationship with my b/f more than anything i have ever experienced. i love my job and the hard work its going to take to keep on growing to the top of my wanted success.

Not everyone sees the complete picture during their first visioning. It may take a few times through the process. Eventually, however, it will come.

It may feel like your life, at this moment, appears to be the opposite of your vision. I guarantee if you work with this vision, study and faithfully apply the principles set forth in this book, your life will begin to look more like what you've written above every day.

EXERCISE: *Building Your Blueprint For Success*

After you've completed the above visioning exercise you will now take that vision and establish it as your intention. Your Blueprint For Success — sometimes called a Treasure Map — is a *physical picture* of your desired reality. It is literally a "visual prayer." Just like a blueprint for a building, this map presents a clear and vibrant image directly to the *right side* of the brain — the part that responds to emotions and images. Science tells us that it is impossible for the right brain to distinguish between an imagined experience and a real one. Thus we are dealing with the creative area of the brain that, as you will learn later in this manual, tends to reproduce in our outer reality that which it accepts as true.

🕐 Give yourself an hour to complete this exercise.

Things you will need:

√   Glue Stick
√   Scissors
√   A variety of magazines
√   Colored poster board:
          —Green for abundance and career success
          —Purple or white for peace and increased spiritual
            understanding
          —Blue for intellectual or artistic accomplishments
          —Orange or bright yellow for health, energy and vitality
          —Red or pink for love, marriage and loving relationships.

Look through the magazines and find pictures that visually represent your desires, then cut them out. They could be pictures of the body you would like to have, or a fabulous car. A good visual aid for increased prosperity might be actual Monopoly money or a picture of a stack of dollar bills. You could choose a painting of a couple embracing or a photo of a confident-looking career woman. It could be a travel brochure photo or a picture of a beautiful home. It might be picture of angels, or individuals you aspire to emulate. Try to use the most colorful images you can find. In addition, you can use words with bright letters (e.g., Success Magazine has "Success" written in big bold red letters.) Use whatever images convey the visual interpretation of your desires fully realized.

Now organize all your pictures on the poster board, using the color that suit your purpose as listed above. Place them in a manner that is pleasing to your eye, then use the glue stick to attach the cut-outs in place. You may also want to draw directly on the board. Some people enjoy replacing the face of the people in the pictures with photos of themselves, making the blueprint even more personal.

When you have finished, regard your Blueprint for Success and declare out loud:

"This is how my inner wisdom sees my life, therefore, it is already established in the invisible. This is my intention which is now blossoming forth into manifest form, right now, peacefully and harmoniously. I rejoice that this, or something better, is manifesting now!"

View your Map while repeating the above affirmation at least twice a day — once when you wake up and once directly before going to sleep. Allow this process to generate feelings of joy and excitement within you. Feel that you *are* this person *now*, that this is your life *now*, this is a present-tense experience rather than a future one. Remember, your creative right-brain cannot tell the difference. Before you know it, things will appear in your life that look amazingly similar to those pictured on your Map. (In my own experience, I was soon given an engagement ring that looked identical to the picture I had put on the board!).

Have fun!!!

CHAPTER TWO

NATURE OF REALITY

*"To see a World in a grain of sand,
and a Heaven in a wild flower,
Hold Infinity in the palm of your hand,
And Eternity in an hour."*
—William Blake

Science and religion are finding more in common every day. Einstein's profound discoveries of the mechanics of the universe, have allowed us to link basic scientific theory with fundamental spiritual concepts.

What science tells us is everything that exits, everything we can see, touch, taste and smell — *everything* in this physical universe — is created out of the *same one substance*, namely atoms. And, all atoms are made up of the *same* exact subatomic particles. You may be wondering, if your hand and the book it's holding are made of the same substance, why do they appear different? The difference is not between the particles themselves, but the *arrangement* of the particles. It is the *intelligence* within the atom that orchestrates the movement of the particles.

With the development of more powerful microscopes, scientists are discovering that the deeper they look into an atom, the larger the spaces are between the particles. Interestingly, scientists estimate that the relative distance between the particles in an atom is greater than the distance between the stars. In fact, they say, the atom is made up of 99.9999% empty space. This empty space is *energy and intelligence.*

Now, if everything is made of atoms and every atom is, in essence, intelligence — then, everything that exists is made of intelligence, the same *one intelligence.* This one intelligence, being non-material in essence, gives rise to, and expresses as, all material forms. There is only one energy and intelligence — and it is omnipresent. This is why we call it a *uni*verse, as opposed to a *di*verse or a *tri*verse. This one intelligence is organized, creative and expresses an immensely intelligent order. In fact, this one intelligence is responsible for creating all that exists and then, guiding and governing all of its creation.

Therefore, if this one intelligence is in all, through all and governs all, could anything exist to oppose it? If there were another power, or force, in the Universe, where would it reside? The fact that there is only one intelligence out of which everything is created, precludes the notion of duality. There are various *aspects* of this one intelligence, and various ways this intelligence behaves, but it's utterly impossible for an opposing power to exist, or for "anti-intelligence" to operate in the universe.

Einstein dubbed this one intelligence that creates, guides and governs the entire universe "the unified field." Religion prefers to call it God. Even though most scientists don't care to admit it, and many religious leaders would rather avoid it, they *are* talking about the same thing. The majority of the world's religions believe that God, the Creator, expresses its beauty through its creations. Many philosophers and sages throughout the centuries have expressed the idea that God is all there is — the one presence and the one intelligence — expressing in a multitude of forms. In the ancient East Indian Upanishads text it is written:

> "Brahman is life. Brahman is joy. Brahman is the Void...
> Joy, verily, that is the same as the Void.
> The Void, verily, this is the same as joy."

Einstein's unified field theory expressed the idea that all are one:

> "We may therefore regard matter as being constituted by the regions of space in which the field is extremely intense...There is no place in this new kind of physics both for the field *and* matter, for the field is the only reality."

Einstein would later declare,

> "I want to know the thoughts of God, the rest are details."

We live, move and have our being in a Cosmos of Intelligence. In his books, Dr. Deepak Chopra insightfully refers to the one intelligence as "the field of all possibilities," describing it as pure potentiality, the absolute which is complete within itself. By definition, the universe contains within itself everything that ever was, is, and will be. It has the ability to express an unlimited number and variety of forms.

This one Cosmos of Intelligence is boundless and without limits of any kind. Can you even begin to conceive of where the Cosmos ends or begins? And what would be on the other side of that? The universe must be unlimited and eternal. Whole unto itself, this Cosmos of Intelligence is life; not simply life as opposed to death, but Life with a capital "L." The infinite number of expressions created from this non-material Life-essence never die or disappear, they only change form. Leaves spring forth, express their beauty until Fall, then turn into brilliantly colored foliage, fall to the ground and give up their form as leaves. In return, the substance of their decay nourishes the ground where they fell, which in turn nourishes that same tree, giving rise to new leaves in the spring. Nothing is wasted. All of life is recycled — same substance, different form.

In this book the term *One Intelligence* will be used alternately with *Universal Intelligence, Universe, Life Force, Spirit, Energy, God* or simply *It*. You will be aware of this because the first letter of each term will be capitalized. Keep in mind however, that the term God (as used within these pages) does not refer to the old idea of an anthropomorphic God as a bearded being seated on his throne in a cloud, looking down on us in judgment. Rather than thinking of God as a separate being, it might be helpful to conceive instead an omnipresent Power of Love, or a Principle of Good in the Universe. It may better serve us to consciously shift our concept of God from a *noun* to a *verb*. If you feel the term Universal Intelligence is too impersonal, simply replace it with the word God in your mind. As you read on, you will recognize that this Power is deeply personal and intrinsically loving. If, on the other hand, you are uncomfortable with the word God, simply replace it with Universal Intelligence. Let's now move on to *qualities* of this Universe.

The Qualities of The Universe

Following is a partial list of the true qualities of the Universe.

The Universe is Abundant

The Universe is inherently abundant because it is limitless, unbounded, and gives rise to an infinite number and variety of forms. To truly grasp the abundance of God, one needs only to look at nature. Consider the number of leaves on all the trees in the world; consider how many grains of sand are on every beach and how many drops of water are contained in all the oceans. Consider how many billions of molecules are in your body and how many billions of stars there are in the universe. The infinite nature of the Universe is truly unfathomable. It is unbounded and unlimited abundance. It is completely self-sufficient and all-providing. The Universe naturally provides for and nourishes all of its creations without exception. This all-providing abundance can be expressed as the *self-givingness* of God.

The Universe is Beauty and Magnificence

Most of us have, at one time or another, gazed upon a beautiful sunset, a rugged shoreline, or contemplated the intricacies of a rose. Remember the feeling that these experiences inspired in you? Perhaps you were struck with a sense of awe? Indeed, it would not be possible for the Universe to create vehicles for Its self-expression as forms that were repugnant to It. All creation is the self-expression of Life's Beauty and Magnificence. It is all around us, from the tiniest ladybug to the vast expanses of the galaxies. In fact, the examples of God's beauty are so plentiful, it would take an eternity to name them.

The Universe is Love

If you've ever looked into the face of a baby, or seen kittens licking each other, or observed a mother suckling her infant, you know how natural and perfect love is. The love that you feel for your spouse, your children, or your dear friends is *an aspect* of the intrinsic Love of the Universe. However, Love is more than an emotion, it is a *power*. Love is a force that is irresistible, unopposable and eternal.

The Universe is Wisdom and Creativity

Being Infinite Intelligence, the universe contains all information, knowledge and limitless wisdom. Also, the extraordinary variety of creation is testament to the limitless creativity which is the essential nature of the Universe.

The Universe is Joy and Happiness

If you've ever watched dolphins cavorting, or young children at play, or squirrels chasing each other around a tree; if you've ever heard birds chirping their songs, or a cat purring, it's easy to understand that joy and happiness are God's perfect plan. You may intuitively sense that when you are in a state of joy, you are in alignment with the perfect order of the Universe. When you are not, you may feel separated.

The Universe is Fulfillment and Success

We can observe this aspect of fulfillment and success in nature every time a plant blossoms, every time a tree bears fruit. This is the natural order of Life. It is the nature of the Universe to come to fruition.

The Universe is Peace, Harmony and Order

From the orchestration of subatomic particles within an atom to the movement of planets in any given solar system, it is quite apparent that the nature of the Universe is harmony and order. Life may at times seem chaotic, but within the chaos there is an underlying purpose. As the poet-philosopher Tagore so beautifully stated: "Every morning the day is reborn among the newly blossomed flowers with the same message retold and the same assurance renewed...that the waves of turmoil are on the *surface*, and the sea of tranquillity is fatherless."

The Universe is Perfection

Webster defines *perfect* as: pure, total, lacking in no essential detail, intact, complete. We may use the same words to describe the universe. Universal Intelligence could not conceive of anything other than Its own perfection. If this were not so, it could not exist. If the Universe were not whole, perfect and complete, it would have destroyed itself eons ago.

These, then, are the essential qualities of the Universe. Since we understand that the Universe is all-inclusive and omnipresent, we may conclude that *all of these qualities are everywhere present*. That means abundance, beauty and magnificence, love, creativity, joy and harmony, peace and perfection are indeed everywhere present at every moment.

Over a century ago, Troward gave us this profound definition of Omnipresence:

"It is therefore, a mathematical necessity that, because the originating Life-principle is infinite, it is a single unit, and consequently, wherever it is at all, the whole of it must be present. But because it is infinite, or limitless, it is everywhere, and therefore it follows that the whole of spirit must be present at every point in space at the same moment."

In other words, there is nowhere these qualities, in their entirety, do not exist. The old adage "There is no place where God is not" is literally true!

Although this is undeniably the absolute truth, it doesn't always appear to us that way. It may seem that there are many places on this planet, in our environment and in our lives that appear imperfect, unloving, less than peaceful or downright ugly. This creates a perception of duality — what is known in metaphysics as the *absolute* and the *relative*. In subsequent chapters, we will explore in detail this apparent duality and, more importantly, how we may transcend it and restore the natural qualities of the universe in our lives.

The Universe Creates

"Thus it is that the Tao produces all things, nourishes them, brings them to their full growth, nurses them, completes them, matures them, maintains them, and overspreads them."

—*Taoism*

As previously stated, everything in the Universe comes from the same one Intelligence and is made of the same substance. Let us now explore how this substance or, non-material essence, becomes material form.

Because non-material essence is intelligence, the process it uses to become form is through and by *active thought* or *intention*. When we think of thought, we are typically thinking in terms of verbally-structured ideas. But there is a larger concept here, one if understood properly, will do nothing less than transform our lives. In essence, *thought is the seed of creation.* In fact, the first thought expressed in the Bible is, "In the beginning was the word."

In order for Intelligence to express itself, it must particularize Itself as distinct form. Being all there is, this Universe must act within and upon Itself. The first action in the process of creation is a *desire* to express Itself as a specific thing; for example, a flower. The desire is the *active thought* of the Universe, which is dynamic. This active thought, or intention, is a creative force that moves upon the inert, omnipresent, non-material essence and becomes a vibration upon this substance. This vibrated, unmanifest substance becomes more and more dense until it is eventually transmuted into manifest form — the flower itself. Intelligence *unformed* becomes intelligence in *specific form* through the activity of thought. The form is seemingly limited, yet its essence is *un*limited. The Absolute expresses Itself by becoming the relative. The Absolute and the relative are simply two sides of the same coin. And, like a hologram, the relative form contains all the intelligence of the Absolute as a whole.

In essence, the manifest universe is the result of the self-contemplation of Universal Intelligence.

Analogy:

You could think of this non-material essence as a fluid substance, such as water. Intelligence has an idea that It would like to express Itself as a beautiful ice crystal. Because this thought is dynamic, it becomes a vibration upon the water (non-material essence) causing molecules to be re-arranged in such a way that it becomes the form of an ice crystal. Intelligence is now expressed as the beautiful crystal. Water can take the shape of many things: ice, steam, power, rain, etc., but it is in *essence* the same substance.

The process is the same with all material expressions. The Universe desires to express Itself as something, for example: a tree, a rose, a rainbow, a waterfall, a planet, or a human being. This desire is a dynamic thought which vibrates upon unformed substance (an aspect of Itself that is completely malleable), becoming formed substance in the exact form that It desires.

> "Creation is only the projection into form of that which already exists."
>
> *--Shrimad Bhagavatam*

Universal Intelligence is *triune* in nature, encompassing the three aspects of existence: the *thinker*, the *unformed substance*, and the *form*. The *thinker* is the creator who "speaks the word" (has the desire), which is an active and dynamic process. The *unformed substance* is subjective and *responsive* to the word. These two aspects of the trinity (thinker and unformed substance) are omnipresent, existing within *and* beyond time and space. The *form* is temporary and, by definition limited, yet it expresses the desire of its creator, and is, in fact, *the word of the creator in manifest form*.

Just as the ice melts back into water, the rose wilts and the rainbow fades, all forms eventually recycle back into the unformed substance from which they came.

> "Molecules dissolve and pass away, but consciousness survives the death of the matter on which it rides."
>
> —Deepak Chopra, *The Way of The Wizard*

Study the Following Chart:

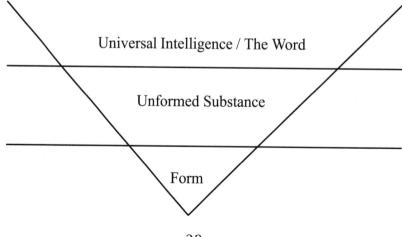

Universal Intelligence / The Word

Unformed Substance

Form

Universal Intelligence, or the word, is the *conscious* part of the Universe. The unformed substance that becomes all form is the *unconscious* or subjective part. The form is the final result of this process. The unconscious part is totally subjective to The Creator and is indeed its servant. It cannot argue, talk back or refuse to become what Spirit wants it to become. The Creator speaks "the word" (dynamic thought) and the Unformed Substance spontaneously becomes the realization of that word. As you can see from the above chart, form *cannot exist without the other two aspects*. All form originates from unformed substance and has behind, and within it, all of Universal Intelligence. This is an Intelligent Universe which becomes the thing it creates, while remaining Universal, Absolute and whole.

> "The Truth is instantaneous in its demonstration, taking only such time in Its unfoldment as is inherent in the law of logical and sequential evolution."
> —*Ernest Holmes*

The manifestation process, while spontaneous in the Absolute, is timebound in the relative physical universe. The manifest universe is more dense than spirit, hence there must be a natural evolution of growth and unfoldment. Yet, the potential is always inherent in the idea. A sunflower is always inherent in the sunflower seed. You must, however, plant the sunflower seed in fertile soil in order for it to blossom into a flower. Also, the sunflower seed will not forget what it is and become a rose by mistake. Intelligence, remember, is an intrinsic component of the seed. In the same way, a thought — or intention — is planted in fertile soil so that it may blossom into its full potential.

Analogy:

In the accompanying illustration, *The Creator* is pictured as a farmer, *unformed substance* as soil, and *form* as the plants. If the farmer's tomato seeds are tucked away in his pocket, they are not given attention, hence would not become tomato plants. If the farmer wants tomatoes, he turns his attention to the seeds (desire) and places them in fertile soil (unformed substance). The farmer doesn't doubt that he will harvest tomatoes or worry that he might get zucchini instead. He's confident that, in a few months, his tomatoes will appear on the vine (manifestation). He knows how they will look and taste, yet they are still only seeds.

EXERCISE: *Nature/Oneness*

Give yourself the gift of a day and go out into nature and contemplate its awesome beauty. Leave behind the city, your current problems and the demands of others. Go to the beach, a nearby lake, the mountains or the desert. The idea is to get as far away from developed land as possible, without sacrificing convenience.

Step 1:

♦ If you are near a body of water, meditate upon it. Close your eyes for a moment and imagine how many drops of this water it would take to fill up a gallon. Now open your eyes and try to consider how many gallons are in the body of water. This is an examples of the unlimited abundance in the Universe. Meditate on the vastness of creation.

♦ If you are in the mountains, choose a vista, sit down and relax. Contemplate how many leaves are on all the trees. Think about how many blades of grass are in the meadows. Then turn your vision upward and contemplate how many square miles of space there are in our galaxy. Meditate on the unlimited abundance in the Universe.

♦ If you are in the desert, take a small handful of sand and try to count the grains in your hand. Next, contemplate how many grains of sand there might be before you. Then, dare to consider how many grains of sand there are on every desert and beach on this planet. If it is a clear night, look up at the sky. Try to count the stars that are in your view of the cosmos. Consider what appears to be one star, may, in fact, be an entire galaxy filled with billions of stars. These are yet further examples of the unlimited abundance in the Universe. Meditate on this.

Step 2:

♦ Wherever you are, hold a water droplet, leaf, blade of grass, or grain of sand in your hand. Consider that it is pure intelligence — a collection of vibrating atoms — specific form that has been created from the unlimited Universal Intelligence which sustains it now. Think of it as Pure Intelligence in a specific form. Now look at your body and see that it too is a collection of vibrating atoms — pure intelligence. Your body is specific form created out of unformed substance by Universal Intelligence, which sustains it now. Now, look around you and recognize that all of nature is *one*. Universal Intelligence expresses Itself in a multitude of forms — yet all are one.

Step 3:

The following poem is by Rabindranath Tagore, an Indian philosopher, poet, musician, educator and trusted friend and advisor to Mahatma Gandhi. Contemplate this beautiful passage:

> "The same stream of life that runs through the world runs through my veins night and day and dances in rhythmic measure...It is the same life that shoots in joy through the dust of the earth into numberless blades of grass, and breaks into tumultuous waves of flowers."

Step 4:

Consider these exercises and express the thoughts that come to you in the space provided below.

_____

_____

_____

_____

_____

_____

_____

_____

_____

_____

_____

_____

_____

_____

_____

_____

C HAPTER T HREE

WHO ARE WE?

"I have said, ye are gods,
and all of you are children of the Most High."
(Psalms 82:6)

In the previous chapter we discussed the creative process of the Universe. Briefly, Universal Intelligence desires, or intends to express as *something* (a tree, a rose, a rainbow, a planet, etc.) and through the process of vibrating upon unformed substance, It becomes formed substance in the exact form of Its intention. This is exactly how the Universe creates and expresses as our physical bodies. However, we are more than our physical bodies. We are triune in nature, reflecting and re-enacting the three-fold nature of Universal Intelligence: Body, Mind and Spirit.

Body

Like all manifest form, your physical body is Spirit in form. Universal Intelligence creates *and* sustains it. Each cell, indeed every atom, is swirling energy and intelligence — Divine Intelligence. The intelligence within each cell communicates with all the other cells at all times. The orchestration of intelligence in our bodies is truly awe inspiring. Consider that there are *three trillion* reactions occurring in our bodies every second! At any given moment, the intelligence in our bodies is pumping blood from our heart into every vein in every limb, digesting the food we eat, converting the oxygen we breathe into usable energy for our cells, killing bacteria, growing hair, perhaps unconsciously tapping our right foot to music, or manipulating our fingers on a keyboard, using our optical nerves to register characters on a page, and perhaps even creating and sustaining an embryo. All of this is happening simultaneously and involuntarily. That's awesome intelligence!

Also, remember that the quality of this Intelligence, or Life Force, is wholeness and perfection. Intelligence cannot express as anything other than it is. Just as water could never change its composition when it is formed into ice (both are hydrogen and oxygen), so too the Life Force could never change its essential nature when it is formed into a physical body. Therefore, the physical body reflects the Universal nature of wholeness and perfection. In subsequent chapters, we will explore why perfection and wholeness do not always seem to be our experience.

Mind

There is only one Mind and that is Universal Mind; It is the mind that is within us. In recent years, there has been a radical shift from the accepted scientific notion that intelligence is located in the structure of brain itself. When Einstein died, his brain was preserved for study. But try as they might, scientists could not find the physical location of his genius. His gray matter looked like every other gray matter. Presently, most scientists tend to agree that genius is not located in the brain — however they are in disagreement as to where else it could be.

We limit ourselves by buying into the tired concept that we were born with only a limited number of brain cells, which determine our level of intelligence. Science is poised to take the next leap of understanding. The truth is, Mind does not have a physical location. Intelligence is omnipresent. We, as individualized expressions of the One Universal Mind, *use* this omnipresent Intelligence. It's as if we were individual terminals linked to the main-frame computer of Universal Intelligence. There is only one Intelligence and each one of us personally *channels* that Intelligence in the amount we *accept* for ourselves. Each of us has access to unlimited genius, which we could utilize *if* we understood how to access it.

Because we all share the same One Mind, all of us are literally connected to one another. Have you ever had an inspired idea and wondered where it came from? You were surprised because it didn't seem to be derived from your personal experience or knowledge-base. ESP and other psychic phenomenon are possible because of the fact that *there is only One Mind*. Have you ever had the sense that something was happening to a loved one without your actually being there? Has it ever happened that a friend came to mind the moment before he or she called? We fool ourselves into thinking we are all separate beings. But, this is not true. Like fingers on a hand, we are all *individual expressions* of this One Mind, inherently interconnected.

> "We lie in the lap of immense intelligence, which makes us organs of its activity and receivers of its truth."
>
> —*Ralph Waldo Emerson*

36

Spirit

What about our Soul or Spirit? The nature of this One Intelligence is love. In order to express Its magnificence, this Infinite Love individualizes as each one of us. I am, you are, and each being is a unique expression of the allness of Universal Spirit. In fact, there is no place where Infinite Love leaves off and we begin. This glorious, omnipresent, Impersonal Life becomes personalized *through* us, *in* us, and *as* us. Who we are, in essence, is Spirit temporarily housed in a physical body. Just as the leaves fall in Autumn, when our time comes, the body will recycle back to the Earth, freeing our Spirit to continue its expression elsewhere. Troward tells us:

> "Infinite as the law itself, is a universal intelligence in the midst of which we float as in a living ocean. Intelligence without individual personality, but which in producing us, concentrates itself into the personal individualities which we are."

Analogy:

We are like waves in a limitless ocean. Each wave is its own self-contained unit, consisting of all the elements of the ocean itself: oxygen, hydrogen, plankton, minerals and sea life. However, an individual wave is not separate from the ocean, it is the ocean expressing as a wave.

~ Or ~

We are like sunbeams radiating out from the Sun. If you view an individual sunbeam shining down on a patch of ground, it looks like a separate shaft of light. But in fact, it is part of a larger whole. Each sunbeam contains all the elements of the Sun and is a necessary part of the Sun. It is the Sun's energy and light in expression.

Life shines forth Its light and energy as the unique being we all are. We are Intelligence in unique expression; the Impersonal, personalized; the Universal un-manifest in manifestation; children of God; Spirit made flesh. Regardless of how you phrase it, *each one of us embodies the full nature of God*. Just as the sunbeam comprises all the elements of the Sun, we comprise all the elements of God. The allness of Life is what we are, always have been, and always will be.

Again, the qualities of the Universe are:

- Love
- Joy and happiness
- Peace, harmony and order
- Beauty and magnificence
- Wisdom and creativity
- Absolute perfection
- Infinite abundance

Therefore, our true nature is love, joy, happiness, peace, harmony, beauty, magnificence, wisdom, creativity, perfection and abundance. Because there is only one Life, there can be no such thing as God *and* something else, there is only God *as*. We can no more be separated from these qualities, than the sunbeam can be separated from the sun.

As you can see, we are far more than just a body with blue, green or brown eyes and blond, brown, or no hair. We are significantly more than our physical characteristics. We are more than our personalities, our family histories, our relationships, our careers, our incomes, our problems, or our illnesses. We are more than we have ever thought we were, and still more than we can possibly imagine.

Consider an iceberg. To those on the surface of the sea, the iceberg may appear enormous, but in actuality they are seeing only a small portion of it. The majority is hidden below the surface, hence the expression "it's just the tip of the iceberg." So too, when we see physical reality, we are seeing only a small part of what is really there — and that part is constantly changing.

Within the non-physical realm, there is a vast dimension of Limitless Intelligence and Immutable Love which comes to a point of personal expression called *you*.

Contemporary Christian mystic, Joel Goldsmith, writes in his book, *Practicing The Presence*:

> "God is our invisible Selfhood: We are the externalized form or expression of that God. God is the creative principle, the source, the activity and the law of our being; and our being is God in expression or manifestation. We as individuals receive our life, law, cause, substance, reality and continuity from the Infinite Invisible, and that invisible activity appears visible as the harmony of our being."

EXERCISE: *Remembering Who You Are*

The purpose of this exercise is to experience your True nature for at least a few moments every day. If you are created out of the image, likeness and very same substance of Universal Intelligence, then all that It is, you are, and all It has is yours now. God's will for you is only what It knows: love, happiness, fulfillment and joy.

1. Move into the silence for a few moments. Close your eyes and take a few deep breaths — in and out.

2. Say to yourself, *"I am an infinite being created out of, and sustained by, perfect Intelligence. I yield to the peace, love and joy that is within me. It is what I am."*

3. Say to yourself: *"I accept God's will of happiness for me. It is what I am."*

4. Repeat the above statement several times. As you do, be cognizant of the fact that because of who and what you are, you have already inherited the Kingdom of Heaven, which includes love, peace, wellness, prosperity and happiness. Heaven has already been established for you. It awaits only your recognition. When you recognize and accept it, it will be re-established in your experience.

Set an intention to repeat the statement in step three every day for one week. Try and remember to say it once every hour during the day. Look at your watch often. Spend thirty seconds every hour remembering who you really are. If you are alone, close your eyes. Say the statement out loud. If you are with others you can keep your eyes open while silently repeating the statement to yourself. Repeat it in the morning upon arising and at the end of the day before falling off to sleep. If a few hours go by and you've forgotten to repeat the statement, don't worry, just begin again at that moment. If negative thoughts should creep into your mind such as, "I don't really deserve to be happy," or "Struggle, sickness and limitation is just a natural part of life," tell these thoughts you will not listen to them anymore. You've had enough of their input throughout your life, and now it's time to try something new. Go back to the statement: *"I accept God's will of happiness for me."*

Practice the above exercise every day for a week as you continue with the following chapters.

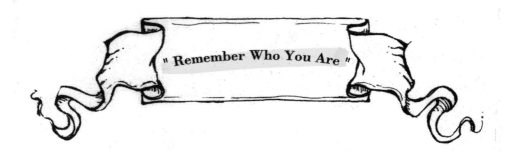

" Remember Who You Are "

CHAPTER FOUR

OUR CREATIVE NATURE

*"The world is saturated with Divinity, immersed in
Reality, and filled with possibility.
We must take this Divine Possibility and mold it
into a present actuality in everyday experience.
This is the way to freedom,
the pathway to peace and happiness."*
— Ernest Holmes

If we are one with the allness of Universal Intelligence then we must also be one with its *Power* — the *creative power* of Universal Intelligence. What distinguishes human beings from the animal kingdom is our ability to self-reflect. We have the capacity to contemplate our existence and imagine various possible futures. This ability to self-contemplate is a powerful tool, for within it lies the capacity to create our lives.

Because we are individualized expressions of Universal Intelligence, we are the natural continuation of the creative process. God creates the universe by Its self-contemplation and *we* create our experience by our *individualized self-contemplation*. God is macrocosm and we are microcosm. In fact, each of us is *an individualized thinking center immersed in this Universal Creative Intelligence*. What's more, the unformed substance, which is all around us, responds to our beliefs and intentions in the exact same way it responds to Universal Intelligence. This is what makes us *"co-creators"* with Spirit.

Originally, the Infinite created us to co-create the beautiful and magnificent...but until we understand this, we will be creating something less than this.

As co-creators, we have all been given individual use of Universal creative power and are using it all the time — *mostly unconsciously.* Just as the Universe creates through Its intention, so are we, as the continuation of this creative process, creating in our lives what *we* believe or intend. If we do not recognize the creative power that is available to us, that in fact responds to us at all times, we may be creating experiences we would rather not have.

Again, examine the chart on page 28. Remember, the unformed substance is subject to the impressions of intelligence. It is there simply to mold the "word" (beliefs and intentions) into form and experience. This is its purpose. *We* are the "intelligence" who speaks the "word" and chooses in *our individual* life. Our beliefs and intentions are like seeds that enter the fertile soil of unformed substance and subsequently bear the fruit of experience in our life.

We are surrounded by, and immersed in, this unformed substance which is powerful to create everything and anything, but has no will of its own — it is

45

neutral. It cannot judge what it thinks would be better for us to experience, then selectively create only that. It must create everything *we* firmly believe and intend. Therefore, *we* supply the will through our beliefs!

It might be helpful to think of this substance as pliant Playdoh-like material. We provide the mold which gives it form. For instance, if we believe we are a failure, we are creating a mold for future failure. The material can only be created in the shape of its mold, and will continue to look the same until *we* decide to change it. Thomas Troward expressed it this way:

> "...therefore what relatively to man, we call his creative power, is that receptive attitude of expectancy which, so to say, makes a mold into which the plastic and as yet undifferentiated substance can flow and take the desired form."

What is our attitude of expectancy? Many of us are accustomed to seeing a world that is dysfunctional and unfulfilling, and because we perceive this to be normal human experience (and thus, normal for us) we misuse the creative power of the Universe, creating negative experiences in our lives. Any condition or experience which is not in alignment with the natural qualities of the Universe are those which *we* have created. Sickness, poverty, limitation, unhappiness, loneliness, struggle, frustration and failure are the result of our *misusing* this One Power. There are not *two* powers (i.e., good and evil), there is only *one* Power and *two ways* of using It. It's not fate. It's not God's will. It's not chance. It's not bad luck. It's not inherited. It's not because you were born under a certain sign. It's not because your house isn't Feng Shui'd properly. As tough as it may be to accept, the Truth is that all limited experiences are the result of what *we* have been *unconsciously* creating.

Ralph Waldo Emerson expressed this idea beautifully when he wrote: "We miscreate our own evils when we interfere with the optimism of nature." The optimism of nature! Nature wants us to be joyous, successful, loving, abundant and express our limitless potential. We interfere with this process when we deny our birthright.

The good news is, once we understand this Truth, it will set us free! We can use the *same power* previously used to create what we *didn't* want, to now create what we *do* want: Love, Joy, Abundance, Fulfillment, Success, Wholeness and Peace. Whereas before we were *unconsciously* creating experiences of struggle and suffering, we will now *consciously* create limitless good in our lives.

Life is a Banquet Table

At the core of our being we are a "field of all possibilities" and we can literally create *anything we can imagine* out of it. The Universe has given us an endless banquet table from which to choose. We can literally *"have it all."* When a beloved Science of Mind teacher explained this principle to our class, she would say, "Trust me, you don't want it all." Because, at this table lies everything — good health as well as sickness, limitless abundance as well as poverty. One can find romance, harmony, peace and joy as well as heartache, chaos, misery and frustration. What choice will we make? *The question really is: what do we accept for ourselves?* Do we accept that loving, harmonious relationships come naturally to us? Or, do we fear that men or women treat us poorly or leave us? Are we accepting that money comes easily to us or do we believe we have to struggle to make ends meet? Do we affirm that life is a stream of harmonious and peaceful experiences or a constant stream of frustrations? Just what are we selecting from this table and putting on our plates? *We* have the Power to choose!

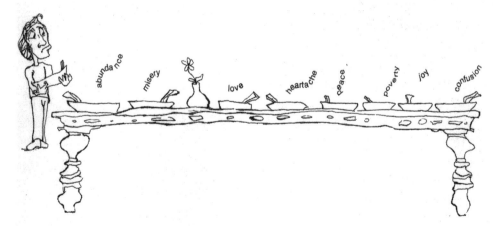

Our experiences in life are simply reflections of what we choose to accept for ourselves. It is our choice that creates our destiny, not our circumstances.

47

Changing The Mold

You can choose to create a new destiny right now. If you do not like the forms this energy has taken in your life, you have the power to change them! Right now, make a commitment to follow these steps:

1. Refuse to give any more power — i.e., your attention — to the forms you do not desire. You were *not* created to fail, be ill, be unhappy, or experience limitation. Neither failure, disease, lack nor misery are the qualities of Love-Intelligence. Do not give your power over to the "miscreation." Refuse to give it your attention. The power is within you — reclaim it! The mold for failure, illness, limitation and unhappiness can no longer hold. *Remember, no form or experience can exist without a belief to sustain it.* It must now dissolve into the nothingness from which it came.

2. Create a new mold. Consciously shift to a new understanding. Focus on your unique gifts. Focus on wholeness — on the limitless abundance in the universe. You were created be successful, vibrant and prosperous, expressing your unique contribution. Fulfillment, wholeness, love and success are what you are, in essence, right now. Claim it and accept it!

3. Remember, unformed substance is responding to your instructions. It can now use the new mold of "success, health, love and prosperity" to begin creating these new experiences for you.

This is a brief overview to get you started. In subsequent chapters, we will explore in depth the process of shifting consciousness from beliefs that no longer serve you to ones that do.

Renewing Our Minds

In the middle 1800s an American mystic by the name of Emma Curtis Hopkins taught spiritual mind healing to many individuals who later became influential leaders in the New Thought movement. One of her insights was:

"My understanding has no form, but it formulates me and my affairs. I have no affairs and no substance except what my understanding formulates."

The Apostle Paul said it simply...

"Be ye not conformed to this world, but be ye transformed by the renewing of your minds." (Rom. 12:2).

We renew our minds by creating a shift in consciousness which transforms *us*, and therefore our experience. When we refuse to accept self-created limitations, and open to an expanded view of ourselves, we become liberated — and as Thoreau said, "...we may live with the license of a higher order of beings."

The Law of Mind

We can also think of unformed substance or creative energy as a law: the "Law of Mind." Spiritual laws are just as predictable and scientific as are physical laws. The Law of Mind is a constant just as the laws of gravity and aerodynamics are a constant. Laws have no opinion about who uses them, or why. They reacts predictably every time, without exception.

Analogy:

The President of the United States has decided to mingle with the people to celebrate his election. You (the ordinary citizen) and the President are standing side by side, toasting his election with two full glasses of champagne. Suddenly, you both drop the glasses simultaneously. They fall to the ground at the same time (assuming they're the same size) and break. The law of gravity does not care that one of you happens to be the President of the United States. His glass falls at the same rate and shatters into pieces just the same as yours. It also does not matter to gravity that these glasses were the most expensive crystal you can buy. They still break.

49

Similarly, the Law of Mind does not care if you believe you are poor and unhappy or abundant and fulfilled. It reflects back to you the conditions and experiences which correspond to your self-acceptance.

The Universe is a giant "yes" machine. It is always saying yes to us. Many believe God does not always answer our prayers. But actually, the Universe cannot help but say "yes" to everything. The question is, what are *we* saying to *It?* The Universe hears our *beliefs* before our *words*. If our prayer is: "Please, God, give me what I need right now," the Universe hears the *belief* that you need, responds by affirming "Yes, you do need it" and answers the prayer by creating experiences which reflect that statement.

Remember, it is done unto us as we *believe*, not as we hope, wish or want. At first, this may seem cruel, but when we realize that the ability to change our lives lies right in our hands — rather, in our beliefs — this becomes the most liberating truth we could ever know. When we embrace a belief system that says, "I am vibrant and healthy," "I am abundant," "I am successful," "I am creative," "I am loved," the Universe hears this belief, affirms "Yes, you are" and answers the prayer by creating experiences which reflect *those* statements.

We must remember that the Universe hears *everything* we say about ourselves all the time, not just when we're repeating affirmations, reading spiritual material, or are in prayer and meditation. Therefore, the question we need to ask is, what are we saying about ourselves the majority of the time?

Example:

Ed is beginning to lose hope that he'll ever find true love. In the past he has been hurt and disappointed by relationships which didn't turn out as he hoped. Every new date is a confirmation that there are no women for him out there. He feels that if he were to meet Ms. Right, she most likely would be spoken for. He still hopes and wishes, but is beginning to feel that loneliness and heartache are his fate in life. It's as if he were pushing away the very thing he desires, simply because, deep down, he believes it's not possible.

Does the Law of Mind take pity on poor Ed? No. The Law is impersonal. Does hoping and wishing work? No. Did God deal him a rotten hand? No. The Universe gives everyone all of Its gifts — and Love, in all its forms is included. Our part is to accept them, *fully*.

Now, let's say Ed begins to recognize that his beliefs may not be serving him — that, in fact, by persistently dwelling on his "problem" he is likely attracting the experience he dreads most. Ed realizes a change in consciousness is due. He begins to give attention to the possibility that Love is already his — embracing the idea that it is indeed his essence. He begins to court the Love within himself and becomes a more loving and giving person as a result. Ed commits to a program of consistently affirming the Truth that he deserves a fulfilling and loving relationship. He begins to feel positive about his life and starts dating again. The women he dates notice there's something special about Ed — he exudes a warmth and confidence. He begins to notice in others what he has found in himself.

Soon he is guided to visit the local bookstore. There, he sees a woman perusing a book by his favorite author. His new-found confidence moves him to speak to her. As it turns out, she is a marvelous woman and is attracted to Ed's warmth and vibrancy. A loving relationship develops and soon they are married.

Now, is this kismet? Has God suddenly taken pity on Ed and sent him a woman? No. The Law of Mind has been operating throughout. It's Ed's consciousness that has changed.

A Law, like any physical law of nature, has no choice but to respond automatically to our input. When you change the input, the Law automatically changes the result. You don't need to *will* anything to happen, or *force* conditions to change. The only effort required is in *changing your mind*. And that shouldn't take effort; *commitment, yes* — effort, no.

Analogy:

Imagine you are in a room. A lamp is plugged into a socket in the wall. This lamp is very old and dingy. The bulb is flickering. The shade is dark and dirty. Imagine the effect of this light on the room. Imagine yourself pulling the electrical chord out of the socket and throwing the lamp into the trash. Now, replace the lamp with a new one and plug it in. This lamp has a 120 watt bulb and a beautiful, translucent, white shade. It's in the *same* socket. It's using the *same electricity* — but the result is completely different! The room lights up like never before.

The law of electricity is a law. It automatically expresses in the form that we give it — no less, no more. It doesn't have an opinion about who uses it and why. The Law of Mind operates in the same way. When we understand this, we can choose to pull the plug on limited thinking. When we don't, the Law continues to create limiting experiences for us. The Law has no choice but to produce the programming we give it.

When we replace "impossibility thinking" with "possibility thinking", the Law is then used to create limitless possibilities of good in our lives.

Spiritual Masters throughout the ages have understood these principles. Adepts, Yogis, Siddhas, Prophets, Messiahs, Enlightened Beings, etc., have either intuitively understood the Power that was available to them, or were initiated into a sacred training. Either way, they learned to harness this Universal Power to instantly manifest whatever was needed in their lives or the life of someone in need. This manifestation took many forms: money, freedom, love, shelter, healing of the sick, fish, bread loaves, etc. These individuals turned away from the wisdom of the time which insisted struggle and suffering were the order of the day. They saw the Universe as the Unlimited Potential for Good, which was available to them. They knew that the same power Infinite Intelligence used to create and maintain the cosmos was the power already within them. They knew that their ability to create by intention, when in alignment with Truth, was the execution of God's will through them. By knowing this Truth, they could simply "speak the word" and their intended desire would spontaneously manifest.

Before you begin to believe that only select individuals are granted special powers, remember that Jesus said: "All these things I do, ye shall do and even greater things shall you do." He wasn't talking about fasting for 40 days, he was talking about *creating miracles!*

Do you have to be an "enlightened master" to create miracles? To spontaneously manifest money in the palm of your hand might take an advanced degree in Yogic training, but to transform a life of unhappiness, loneliness and failure into a celebration of joy, fulfillment, love and success, is entirely within your reach. And, you don't have to meditate for years in the Himalayas to achieve it! In fact, you can begin to use these principles with your current level of understanding. You can start now by practicing with the following exercises.

EXERCISE: *Re-Creating Your Experience*

1. Think about a situation which tends to engage either your fear, feelings of inadequacy, anger or resentment. What circumstance makes you feel small in some way? Re-create the experience in your mind. Think about what you're doing and saying in this situation. What do you perceive others are thinking, doing and saying? What sort of feelings does this circumstance bring up for you?

   For example: Monique is a talented artist who paints colorful, inspiring canvases. Her artistically inspired visions flow through her as fast as she can get them onto canvas. However, she has tremendous difficulty promoting herself and her work. She knows that the only way her work will sell is by generating publicity for herself and by getting to know gallery owners. It is her *perception* that an artist must be highly praised by all the "important" art critics for any gallery to take him or her seriously. Since she's yet to be reviewed by any "important" art critic she feels inadequate. She procrastinates when it comes to making the calls she needs to make. When she finally gets up the nerve to call a gallery she becomes a bit nervous. Her hands sweat and her voice sounds timid and shaky. The person she's talking to would like to get enthusiastic over her work but yawns instead and tells her to send her slides and they'll "get back to her."

2. Now, take the situation you've chosen and walk through it in your mind — but this time, from a *higher perspective*. This time, call upon your God-given gifts of wisdom, confidence, love, peace, joy and enthusiasm to carry you

though. Remember you are God's beloved and the Universe is *for* you. Imagine that this situation now engages your competent, loving and genius qualities instead of pressing your "inadequate buttons." Feel yourself in the scenario; hear yourself talk, see what you do, explore how you feel, observe how others respond.

For example, in Monique's case, she would first remind herself that she's extremely talented with a valuable gift to share with the world. She affirms that her art is capable of inspiring others and brightening homes with beauty. Her artistic gift is indeed a blessing to others. She builds her enthusiasm for sharing information about her art with reviewers and galleries. She now visualizes herself making the call. She feels confident, centered, poised, enthusiastic and articulate as she talks with others about her work. She remembers that each person she speak with is an expression of the same Love-Intelligence which is within her. Monique consciously unifies with this presence within the person on the other end of the phone. She observes them catching her enthusiasm and responding with eagerness. It's a joyful communication. Monique does this process first in her mind. When it feels complete, she opens her eyes and actually makes the call she's been procrastinating about.

You can do this exercise right before any challenging situation. You'll be amazed at the transformation in yourself and the experience. Suddenly, something that used to make you feel small is now empowering.

EXERCISE: *The Parking Spot*

Not being able to find a parking spot these days is a universally frustrating problem. You know the feeling — you're at a sporting event, concert, or strip mall with an inadequate number of spaces. You drive around, looking for a spot, wasting time. Maybe you've just spotted one when someone suddenly pulls in before you. The next time you're in a similar situation, say this to yourself:

> *"I know that in this Universe there is a perfect place for everyone including myself. As I silently send love to everyone here, I am align-*

54

ing myself with the Creative Power of the Universe. I know that there is a perfect vacant spot for me and Universal Intelligence is now guiding me to it. I give thanks, and so it is.

Visualize that empty spot and *believe* you are being guided to it. If the Universe can direct the course of the stars, it can certainly lead you to a parking spot!

Remember, if the universe is *for* us,
who or what can be against us?!

CHAPTER FIVE

ATHENTIC SELF

&

FALSE SELF

"Unhappy is he who mistakes the branch for the tree, the shadow for the substance."
—*The Talmud*

As expressions of the Infinite, it is natural for us to be loving, joyous, happy, fulfilled, peaceful, successful, abundant and perfect. So why doesn't that seem to be our everyday experience? Two passages from the Bible may give us a clue.

"And God said, Let us make man in our image, after our likeness."
(Genesis 1:26)

"God hath made man upright, but they have sought out many inventions"
(Eccl. 7:29)

Though stated in Biblical terms, the first statement is scientifically accurate. If there is one Universal Intelligence from which all creation originates, then we cannot possibly be created as anything *other* than in Its "image and likeness." As mentioned previously, the qualities of this Universal Intelligence are love, joy, happiness, peace, harmony, abundance and perfection. How could God create anything *unlike* Itself? *It can't.* Therefore, in truth, we are all individualized expressions of pure love, pure joy, complete happiness, limitless peace, harmony, exquisite beauty, magnificence, absolute perfection and unbounded prosperity. This is how we were created and what we are in Truth. Let's call this our "authentic self."

Now, here's the variable: we are given an important gift at inception, and that is *freedom of choice.* We have the choice to agree with the inherent truth of our being and live our lives from that awareness, or we have the choice to disregard it, ignore it, and push it away. Emerson stated: *"...we but half express ourselves and are ashamed of that divine idea which each of us represents."* Mostly, though, it's not such a conscious choice. Since most of us are born into families that have forgotten they are the self-expression of the Infinite, they unknowingly pass this misinformation on to us as children. We grow up believing that we are separate from our Source, separate from the Love-Intelligence which created us, and inherently inadequate. When we disregard the truth that we are beings created "in the image and likeness" we, by default, "re-create" or "re-invent" ourselves in another image — *a distorted* image.

"Freedom is not worth having if it does not include the freedom to make mistakes."
— Mahatma Gandhi

We have the freedom to make mistakes and we've made an egregious one. We have made the mistake of *forgetting who we are*. We are asleep to our inherent magnificence. The error is compounded by "inventing" a counterfeit self to replace our authentic self. We'll call this counterfeit self the "false self." Some refer to it as the ego. However, so as not to confuse the reader with traditional psychology's definition of *ego*, the term *false self* will be used instead.

The false self was born from a belief that we are separate from our Source, separate from our good and separate from each other. The false self incorporates a belief structure which includes the assumption that we are powerless, subject to the winds of fate, a victim of circumstance, alone, empty and unloved. Generation after generation has erroneously assumed that this false self is true human nature. We tend to accept, without question, that the false self is who we are for two reasons: a) it is what we were taught from the moment we were born, and b) society constantly reinforces this assumption. It's not the Truth of us, but we *believe* it is — because until we discover otherwise, it's all we know.

A Troubled Sleep

How could we all be fooled by an identity which is not truly us? When did we fall asleep to the Truth of who we really are? This a mystery to which no one has definite answers. These are questions to be taken inside and asked of your inner wisdom. My answer may not be "the answer," but, it is what my inner wisdom tells me is true. I'm sharing it here as one possible hypothesis.

Eons ago, at a certain point in Earth's evolutionary cycle, we "spirit-beings" incarnated as human beings to express Divine Love and experience life on this Earth-plane. At that time, we lived as the Universe intended: peaceful, loving, prosperous beings, living in the material world, yet fully aware of our spiritual essence. We lived, moved and had our being in Spirit. We lived in harmony with one another, and with the realization that we could create for ourselves anything we needed from the limitless, invisible Source. Over time, because of the density of the physical world, we began to lose our interest in the subtleties of our spiritual essence. Simply put, form became more appealing. We became enamored by the variety of forms which we created through the manifestation process. So much so, that we began to forget the Intelligence behind the form. Because we were losing the focus on our spiritual identity, we began to

60

identify ourselves as a physical body. We began to notice differences in body types and skin color. As soon as this occurred, we began to feel a sense of separation from our brothers and sisters. Judgment of others quickly followed suit.

It was only a matter of time that we developed the notion we were separate from our creator, our Source. The memory that we were an integral part of Universal Intelligence was lost, and we began to believe in a God which was located outside of us. We forgot we were co-creators and began to believe life just *happened to us.* We believed that we were victims of fate and judged things and experiences as "good" or "bad." We created a God in *our* image and likeness. We assumed he judged *us* as good or bad and doled out, or withheld, his gifts accordingly. Consequently, we developed an erroneous concept that we were "sinners," deserving of punishment. We began to feel guilt, shame and fear. We judged others and then loved or withheld *our* love accordingly. We developed a protective, defensive and fearful way of interpreting life. We forgot that our fulfillment came from our connection with the Infinite Source within us and then flowed out into our lives. As a result we felt empty and began to crave things, people and substances in the outer world in order to make us feel full. Because we lost our sense of inner *fulfillment*, we began to crave *"fillfulment."* Addictions, obsessions and many forms of dysfunctional behavior developed as a natural consequence.

These erroneous perceptions gave birth to the false self which eventually robbed our awareness of the authentic self. *This* was our "fall from grace."

For most of us, this "false self" has become our dominant self today, and our authentic self is only glimpsed from time to time. It can be said that the false self has served humankind by allowing us to maneuver our way through the confused world which we've invented. However, the potential to express the authentic self remains within us at every moment. Of one thing we can be sure: each of us enters this incarnation with the longing to wake from the ego dream and once again live in the full awareness of our authentic self.

A Spiritual Revolution

Throughout time, there have been those few masters, sages, saints and yogis who have caught a glimpse of the authentic self and, refusing to live in a world of illusion, have dedicated their lives to its expression. It is now time for *us* to awaken from the dream that we are separate from our Source. We must finally open our eyes and gaze upon the Kingdom of Heaven, which is our true home. It is the Father's good pleasure to give us the Kingdom, but *we* must do the accepting. Thus, there are *two* parts to this spiritual principle. The gift has already been given, but, the gift is not complete until it has been accepted and embraced.

There is a quiet "spiritual revolution" taking place in the world today and one day everyone will remember who they truly are. It's not a question of *if,* but *when.* So, why wait for it to be the "popular and accepted" belief? Why delay your good? Why not begin to benefit from an awakened life now?

Many will wait, perhaps several lifetimes, to choose the expression of their true identity. A limitless life frightens those who have a vested interest in keeping things "the way they are." Living life with the false self at the helm works for many people — for a time — until the pain of separation becomes intolerable. Wholeness is an experience we all instinctively crave and it cannot be denied much longer.

So, instead of being in the large group of the "blind following the blind," you can rise above the pack as a leader. You can change your experience of this world in this very moment. You can *choose* to discover your authentic self and express it's magnificence. Not only will your own life be transformed, but you will serve as a light to guide others out of darkness.

> "Why wait for heaven? Those who seek the light are merely covering their eyes. The light is in them now. Enlightenment is but a recognition, not a change at all."
>
> —*A Course in Miracles*

The Two Selves

The false self has an existence because we've giving it one. It exists within us simultaneously alongside our authentic self. The self to which we give our power is the one that is dominant. When one self is dominant, the other is recessive. The first step in making the shift from expressing the false self to the authentic self, is to distinguish the difference between the two. Once we've

62

understood how the two selves operate, it will be easier to make the choice to shift.

The best way to detect whether the false self is operating is to observe our thoughts and feelings. When we are in alignment with the false self, the feelings we have may be obvious, or subtle and difficult to pin down. We may simply feel a lack of aliveness and vibrancy, an edginess or a feeling of being incomplete. We may feel inadequate, unworthy or small. We might have a sense of emptiness, and try to fill ourselves up with things in the outer world in a compulsive way. Not realizing the false self is in control, we may feel compelled to, for instance, eat too much, drink too much, spend too much, do too much, or talk incessantly, etc. We crave *something* to fill up the empty hole we feel inside, or to at least distract us long enough so we won't notice that we're not express-ing our True nature.

When we are in alliance with our false self, we tend to judge ourselves and others. We may focus on our own flaws and begin to compare ourselves to others. We may suffer from feelings of inferiority. We may become critical of someone's behavior or even their appearance. We overlook the beauty and mag-nificence which is innately within a person, particularly when they're not ex-pressing it at the time.

The false self is confused. It relies on outward conditions to identify itself, or to puff itself up, i.e., "I'm terrific because I have a nice car," or "I'm important because I have an important sounding title," or "I'm worthy of atten-tion because I have a beautiful wife, or my kid made the honor roll." There's nothing wrong with these things in and of themselves, however, the problem arises when we rely on external conditions to measure our worth. Not only that, but, outer conditions are in a constant state of flux. This individual's child may get into trouble next year, or his wife could leave him, or he may be sacrificing what he really wants to do for a living. He may be giving up what truly makes his heart sing, in order to have that important title which society has told him will make him happy. When we believe we *are* our achievements or our failures, what we have or don't have, how our body looks or doesn't look, then we are identifying with the false self.

No matter how great you can make your body look, how many degrees you can earn, how many things you can acquire or accomplish, or how "perfect" you can make your life look; none of it will ever make you feel fulfilled or truly happy while you believe those "things" define who you are. It will always be based on a false notion that wholeness is not already within you and that are you are in need of being fixed. Trying to fill an empty hole that is bottomless, only gives you the *illusion* that the more you stuff into it the more the emptiness will go away. This is a common mistake many people who are on the "personal growth" track make. It is the "I need to fix me because I'm not okay now" syndrome. They get caught on a wheel of suffering that does not end until they choose to experience a life lived from the awareness of the authentic self.

No matter what form it takes, the only problem we ever have
is an *identity problem*.

Reverend Nirvana Gale once told our class, "You are not a work in progress, you are a masterpiece unfolding." The awareness that you are a masterpiece unfolding is the awareness of the authentic self which lives in a different world than that of the false self. Being aligned with the authentic self is to be centered in the recognition that, because you are the self-expression of Universal Intelligence, you are inherently beautiful, perfect, magnificent and complete. You do not need to acquire or accomplish anything to become this. You simply need to acknowledge that you are "It" already.

When you come from the awareness that you are already complete, the manifestation of your heart's desires is a simple and natural process. Instead of determining your self-worth by your accomplishments, when you come from the awareness of your authentic self, your accomplishments are a natural expression of who you are. Do you see the difference? The shift in perception appears subtle, yet the transformation in your life will be radical.

The authentic self is the place of power, peace and limitless love within you. Your authentic self is fully connected with the Source at all times. This higher consciousness has never been hurt, harmed or endangered in any way. Yes, it has experienced the exact same situations you have (after all it is you) only it has perceived them differently.

When you are in alignment with your authentic self you are centered in the flow of Life itself. You are automatically expressing your potential in every area and performing each task at your peak level. You move in the world on purpose and in the direction of your vision. Obstacles are seen as mere stepping stones toward your good. You recognize that you are inherently blessed and you see everyone else the same way. There is a radiance about you that originates from behind your eyes and touches all with whom you come into contact. It is an *attractive* energy which draws positive people and experiences to you. Your authentic self is also your intuitive voice; it is the seat of all inner wisdom and insight.

The following is a sampling of qualities from both selves:

False Self	*Authentic Self*
-Feels separate and alone	-In alignment with Source
-Fearful	-Loving and compassionate
-Feels inadequate, unworthy	-Joyous, radiant, powerful
-Feels empty, tries to fill the "hole"	-Knows its own wholeness
-Identifies with outer circumstances	-Committed to fulfilling its vision
-Struggles / Ineffective behavior	-Obstacles become stepping stones
-Judges/condemns self & others	-Forgives
-Self-sabotages	-Expresses its potential
-Feels it is a victim	-Voice of intuition & divine guidance
-Feels guilt and shame	-In the flow, in the Zone, peak experience

This authentic self is known by a variety names: inner Self, inner Christ, Higher Self, the Observer, the soul, and superconciousness among others. Ralph Waldo Emerson referred to it as the Oversoul. It doesn't matter what you call it, the point is to *call upon it*. Invite your true self to reveal itself to you and through you.

You are a *unique being*. There is no one else who expresses in your special and beautiful way. You have a divine purpose and were created to do something that has not been realized in quite the same way. No one else has your special gift. When you are in alignment with your authentic self, you are automatically in your "right place," and where you stand is holy ground. "Ye are the light of the world," the Master teacher instructed us. When you are able to let go of the false self, you will allow the light of your authentic self to shine in the world!

The Perennial Story

The false self struggles for recognition and domination over our authentic self. While it may be controlling our behavior a majority of the time, it can never usurp our true self, which is our divine identity. Ultimately the false self will be seen for what it is — *our creation.* The authentic self, if we allow it, will ultimately prevail. This is the archetypal story of the struggle of good over evil that has been with us since there were people to tell it. It has had as many interpretations as there are interpreters. A good, juicy drama is a engaging experience. It fascinates us. Perhaps because we so enjoy a good drama, we give power to something that has no inherent reality.

The only reason "good" appears to *struggle* over "evil", is because we consider evil to a legitimate part of the working universe. If there is only one Power and Intelligence from which all is created, *evil cannot exist.*

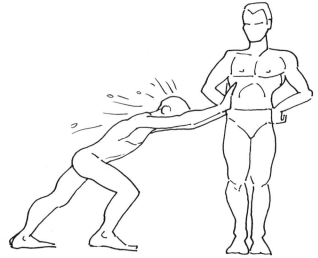

When we fully realize the non-reality of the false self, its shadow will fade to nothingness. No struggle is required in the process, only a commitment to train ourselves to recognize the false self — then re-align with the authentic self.

Self-Worth

The most insidious way the false self robs us of the magnificent life we were meant to live, is by questioning own sense of self-worth.

For example, let's say you're now open to the manifestation of your heart's desires and are committed to fulfilling your vision. You are inspired by your inner guidance and are moving forward. You might ride this wave for a while confident that you are truly magnificent and have a superb gift to express to the world. You acknowledge that you indeed deserve limitless good. You move in the world on purpose. Then suddenly, out of the blue, a fear thought bubbles to the surface. Perhaps you encounter a road block which appears insurmountable. Unexpectedly, that old self-doubt returns to haunt you. You may hear yourself saying, "What was I thinking, I can't do that! Who do I think I am? I don't know enough about that, or I don't have the right education or training to do that." You might begin to doubt that you're too old to start that now, or you're not smart enough, talented enough or good looking enough. You may feel you don't have enough resources, or you might begin comparing yourself to others who appear to have more of "an advantage." Perhaps your fear is that if you followed your guidance, manifested abundance or expressed your magnificence, your friends wouldn't like you anymore because they'd think you're better than *they* are. Maybe you subconsciously fear no longer fitting in with your peers. Perhaps you *have* achieved something, or expressed your authentic self in a new way, but you insist that it wasn't especially important. By doing so, you minimize the importance of your own growth. On the other hand, maybe you begin to blame others for not supporting you the way you would like. Perhaps you get angry or push away those who love you.

Regardless of the form your self-doubt takes, it's evident the false self has stepped in and wants to stop your unfoldment. After all, if you express your authentic self, where does that leave the false self? — ignored and eventually annihilated.

As a self-surviving technique, the false self must introduce the issue of worthiness, which in turn sabotages the manifestation of our good. When we feel, deep down, that we don't really deserve fulfillment — when we continually *and subconsciously* question our own sense of self-worth — we have let the false self rule. If we continue to listen to the voice of the false self, we interfere with the natural process of fulfillment we had worked so hard to accept.

The tricky part is, feelings of unworthiness are just below the level of our consciousness. We're generally unaware of their existence. Nonetheless, these subconscious feelings contribute to our lack of success. Before we realize the false self is in control, our train comes to a stop and we don't follow through on our inspiration. We may suddenly become sidetracked, finding reasons why our desire is unrealistic. We may begin to listen to those family members and friends who tells us we're crazy. We may begin to buy into the notion that a life which is less than fulfilling is normal — and we should be content with it. We become easily distracted, or we simply can't seem to find the time to implement our plans. We become lazy and allow our minds to slip back into limited thinking. What's more confusing is that the more we begin to expand and "step out in trust", the louder this voice of doubt becomes.

We can put a halt to this cycle of self-sabotage. We can learn to eradicate the voice of the false self and begin to see it for what it is — simply our own invention.

The false self feeds off our *unawareness* of it. Identifying the ways in which we stop our own natural unfoldment increases our awareness. The moment we become cognizant that our false self is in control, the spell is broken. A loving mother reveals reality by turning on her frightened child's bedroom light. The child now rests in confidence knowing there are no monsters under the bed. Similarly, to reveal our true self-worth, we simply need to lovingly shine the light of awareness on the false self which masquerades as us. This shadow self, complete with its doubts and fears, will then disappear before the light.

"Nothing real can be threatened. Nothing unreal exists."
                                        —*A Course in Miracles*

"The unreal hath no being; the real never ceaseth to be."
—*The Bhagavad Gita*

Exercise 1: *Define the difference*

Everyone experiences their false self in different ways. Identifying your feelings and behavior will help you determine when it is in control.

1a. Five ways I *feel* when I am in alignment with my false self:

_____

_____

_____

_____

_____

1b. Five ways I *behave* when I am in alignment with my false self:

_____

_____

_____

_____

_____

2a. Five ways I feel when I am in alignment with my *authentic* self:

_____

_____

_____

_____

_____

2b. Five ways I *behave* when I am in alignment with my authentic self:

_____

_____

_____

_____

_____

Exercise 2: *Making The Shift*

Step 1

        You may be aligned with your false self for some time before you recognize that it's actually running you. That's okay. As you progress you will learn to catch it earlier each time. The moment you *do* realize you're in alignment with the false self, take a moment for yourself, in private if possible. Without judgment and with an emphasis on self-love, communicate to yourself something similar to the following.

"I've been under the impression that I could be separate from my Source. I've simply made a mistake in my identity, believing that I was alone and apart from my good. I forgot for a moment that who I truly am is the self-expression of Pure Love, Joy, Peace and Magnificence Itself. I forgot for a moment that I am a beloved child of the Universe which fulfills Itself as me. I forgot for a moment that I am complete now, and all I ever need is within me. I forgot for a moment that I have a unique and beautiful gift to give the world."

Step 2

Affirm your commitment to expressing your authentic self as follows:

"This moment I call forth my authentic self to be fully expressed. This moment I invoke the loving, joyful, confident, creative, powerful, radiant self which is my true essence to reveal itself. (Call forth whatever qualities of your authentic self you would like to have expressed now.) I let go and let my authentic self lead the way."

Step 3

Move into action. Do something you know is in alignment with your authentic self. Some examples are:

- Tell someone you love them.

- Look in the mirror and tell yourself: "I love you!"

- Go for a jog, or do some other physical activity which brings you pleasure.

- Allow your creativity to express through writing, drawing, singing or dancing.

- Pick up your favorite hobby and do whatever that is for 30 minutes.

- Make that phone call you've been putting off.

- List the ways you can turn an obstacle into a stepping stone.

• List five things you can do to achieve a goal — and then do one of them.

Whatever the action, always remember to begin the activity with an awareness that it is your *authentic self* which is stepping forward.

Exercise 3: *Journal*

Another tool to assist you in making the shift from your false self to your authentic self is through the process of journaling.

Step 1

If the false self feeds off unawareness, our healing will occur when we become aware. The most effective way to do this is by journaling. Journaling is an excellent way to catch those doubts before they result in self-sabotaging behavior.

If you feel your train is coming to a stop, or you're losing interest in something that had fired your very spirit only a short while ago, you can be sure there is something going on just below the level of consciousness where the false self hides. If you're encountering obstacles which are becoming increasingly difficult to overcome, or you find yourself listening to someone who insists your idea is a bad one, or you have a nagging sensation that you're not good enough, smart enough, disciplined enough, etc., to have your dreams fulfilled, then it's time to sit down and start journaling.

The best time to journal is upon rising in the morning. But if that's not possible, find another time — maybe late in the evening, before bed. As the Nike slogan goes: "Just do it." Take pen in hand and put it to paper. Let the thoughts flow like a stream of consciousness. Don't censor. You may even want to begin the journaling session with a question, i.e., "Why am I suddenly feeling unworthy? or "What is it that's stopping me?" Then allow your intuitive self to answer that question by using your hand to write. Don't be afraid to explore the voice of the false self. Remember, it will only hurt you if you remain unaware of it. Why is it telling you you're not good enough? Are those reasons absolute Truths, or simply perceptions?

Step 2

Now, in your journal ask the question, "Who am I really?" Allow your thoughts to be guided by that place of limitless Love within you. Create a list of reasons why you are worthy of having what you desire. List all your strengths, talents and assets. Explore the truth that you do indeed deserve love, abundance, peace, joy, health, success, prosperity and fulfillment because it is your divine inheritance!

Remember, you are building a new muscle. It requires the same attention and repetition as building your biceps would. Stick with it, the rewards are tremendous. As you learn to shift your attention and your power to the authentic self, you will automatically wipe out a host of problems that were caused by identifying with the false self. Although it may appear you have many problems, in truth you have only one, and that is *forgetting who you truly are*. Once you've developed the muscle to express your authentic self, problems you assumed were difficult to solve clear up on their own accord.

Reverend Joan Steadman wrote the following insightful passage for the December '96 issue of *Science of Mind Magazine:*

"It takes courage to relinquish smallness and be willing to express our unlimited potential. Such a way of life may seem overwhelming, yet we can always remember that we, of ourselves, do nothing; rather, the indwelling Presence accomplishes the appointed task. In true humility, we trust that we can fulfill the greatness of our divine purpose by the power of God that lives, moves, and has its being as us. Our spiritual mandate is to allow God to be God as us in all of Its magnificence and glory. It's up to us to accept this great and noble charge, to say yes to the impulse of Spirit that is always yearning to express more and more as us."

[The exercises in this chapter were inspired by the work of Professional Life & Career Coach, Rhonda Britten.]

C HAPTER SIX

CORE BELIEFS

"It is done unto you as you believe."
(Mt. 8:13)

As stated in the previous chapter, many deeply held beliefs we have about ourselves and our world stem from the original mistaken concept that we are separate from our Source, separate from our good and separate from each other. We were born into this belief system which has been reinforced by our culture, and now accept it as our reality. This deeply rooted sense of separation gives rise to a variety of erroneous core beliefs. These beliefs are *perceptions* of how life works, and are not necessarily *facts*. At first glance many perceptions *appear* to be true — we can even quote statistics to support them — but upon closer examination we find they are not inherently factual and, more importantly, need not be true for us. Consider the following examples of common erroneous core beliefs:

- Life is hard and then you die
- The odds are against you
- All good things must come to an end
- You must compete to get ahead
- You have to work very hard to make enough money to live comfortably
- Good single men (women) are hard to find
- Romance dies after marriage
- True love is found only in fairy-tales
- The older I get, the more prone to illness I am
- There's not enough to go around

Or, any variation of the "I'm not enough" syndrome, such as:

- I'm not educated enough, rich enough, talented enough, young enough, well enough, thin enough, etc., to do, or have what I desire.

You can probably add a few of your personal favorites to this list. Many of these core beliefs have been with us a long time and are deeply rooted in our subconscious. Imagine a record album which has a groove deeply scored in the vinyl. Every time the record is played, the needle falls automatically into that groove. In the same way, our core beliefs may be deeply etched in our consciousness, and our minds slip into those grooves automatically.

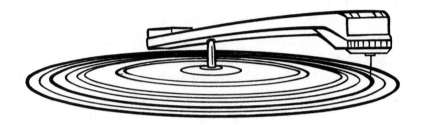

Example:

Brenda has always wanted to have her own business. She's had numerous innovative ideas for new ventures, so many that her friends have dubbed her "the idea lady." Trouble is, each time she considers putting one of her ideas into action, her mind automatically goes to either "Most small businesses fail in the first few years" or "I don't have enough business education to manage it correctly" or "I don't have enough capital to make it happen, and what bank is going to give me a loan?" Brenda stops herself from acting before she even begins. Her heart is telling her that having her own business would express her potential and be a joyous, fulfilling experience, but she pulls back every time.

She can't even *consider* taking a business course to bone up on her skills, or doing some market testing, or having someone help her write a business plan so she can present it to a potential investor. She can't get this far, because her erroneous core beliefs arrest any further consideration. So, she pushes her innovation aside and stands on the sidelines, watching someone else bring her ideas to life.

No matter how long these erroneous core belief have been with us, no matter how deeply implanted they are in our subconscious, they *can* be uprooted. The process of uprooting begins with identifying the erroneous core beliefs as mere perceptions, then discovering the Truth which is hidden behind them. When we shift our core beliefs from *perception* to *Truth* we see the world and ourselves from a higher perspective. Viewing our world from this vantage-point transforms our experience of it.

Shifting Core Beliefs in The Collective Unconscious

We human beings have many prevailing perceptions we share as a culture. These perceptions are the prevalent beliefs our society accepts as true, generally without question. Psychologist Carl Jung described this phenomenon as "the collective unconscious." Ernest Holmes called it "race-mind consciousness" (referring to the human race). Many of these shared perceptions form the basis of our *human* awareness. If we do not make the effort to question whether or not a perception is actually true, it will automatically become part of our belief system and, consequently our experience.

Just as we can shift our individual core beliefs, those of the collective unconscious can also be shifted. History is our best example of this. Examine the following:

Examples:

♦ There was a time we believed it was impossible for a human being to run a mile in less than four minutes. It was universally acknowledged that the human body was physically incapable of the challenge. Then, Roger Bannister came along and ran it in 3:59. Suddenly the limitation was removed. Since then, runners have been steadily breaking Bannister's record. In fact, running the mile in 3:59 is now considered slow.

♦ We once thought no one would ever land on the moon. In fact, believability standards were set by this core belief, thus the phrase, "Why, I could afford to buy that house about as easily as I could go to the moon!" Then President Kennedy announced on television his intention to send a manned space craft to the moon — before the Russians. We now had a strong national purpose for achieving this goal. The American people believed Kennedy, and his intention became ours. Keep in mind that the technology for such a mission had not been developed yet! Nonetheless, a*s soon as we believed we could*

79

do it, we found the way.

♦ Ten years ago, medical professionals insisted it was rare for women over 40 to give birth to their first child. It was widely believed that a woman's child-bearing years were in her twenties. However, since the rise of the women's movement, many women have chosen to delay parenthood to have a career. As a result, the needs of women have created an expanded consciousness. We refuse to accept the "fact" that an older pregnancy is impossible. Again, in response to the change in consciousness, technology has risen to the occasion. Consequently, in the last decade, births to women over 39 have increased by more than fifty percent. Fertility medicine is one of the fastest growing fields in medical science. Recently, women in their 40's and even 50's have been giving birth to healthy babies. Today, it's not only possible, it's a common occurrence. Looks like they'll have to update those textbooks.

In each of the above examples, as the individual or group involved refused to accept the current limitation, they collectively shifted from "impossibility thinking" to "possibility thinking". As a result, they *experienced* freedom and success rather than limitation and powerlessness.

Roger Bannister wrote the following about his experience:

"No longer conscious of my movement, I discovered a new unity with nature. I had found a new source of power and beauty, a source I never dreamt existed."

Herein lies the key. When we connect with that Source of Power which is within us, it will expose limiting core belief for what they are — self-imposed. This exposure to Truth will render them powerless.

Healing Erroneous Core Beliefs

Discovering and *correcting* limiting core beliefs is absolutely essential if we want to manifest our desires on a permanent basis. If we set our intention to manifest a specific desire while harboring a core belief that insists it's impossible, the good we create will be, at best, *temporary.* Simply repeating a positive affirmation such as, "I am prosperous" without first eliminating the underlying, negative core belief that there's not enough to go around, is akin to slapping a Band-Aid on a festering wound. The wound will not heal until we treat it.

In treating a negative core belief, it is necessary to first look at it. We must ask ourselves the following questions: What limitations have I been accepting without question? Is this belief a fact, or a perception? Is it originating from my false self, or from the collective unconscious? Just because it seems to be a prevalent experience, does this perception need to be true for me? The process of recognizing our negative core beliefs can be a challenge because it's often difficult for us to be honest with ourselves. But, brutal honesty is exactly what it takes. As Emerson tells us: "God will not have his works manifest by cowards."

We live in a world that repeatedly tells us our good is limited and we're powerless against the forces of illness and misfortune. It tells us life is a crap shoot, and most businesses and marriages fail. It tells us that only a few individuals have the power and it's those who will ultimately determine our fate. It tells us we need to aggressively compete with each other in order to win in the game of life. It tells us to grab for what we can, because there's not enough to go around. This world tells us to fear our neighbors and to be suspicious of everyone we meet. No wonder we're terrified of trying anything new, be it a relationship or career change. This is why, even when good appears in our life, we tend to sabotage it. After all, our core beliefs tell us, "who are we to deserve it?" "Why should we be successful in every area of our lives? It's unnatural." In addition, the world around us reinforces these beliefs, making then even more welcome in our consciousness. We have accepted these pernicious lies for so long they have become our reality. A commitment to heal these intoxicating beliefs is what is needed if we truly want to be free of limiting experiences.

"If we do not like the world we live in, then we do not like our thoughts."
—*Emma Curtis Hopkins*

Right now you may be saying, "I can't possibly be responsible for creating *all* of the chaos or unhappiness in my life!" Well, yes and no. It is a fact that what we accept as true about ourselves manifests as experiences in our world.

So, in that sense, yes, we are responsible. However, we may not have placed the belief there in the first place, and may not even be aware of its existence.

When we're not consistently mindful, many of the beliefs and assumptions of the collective unconscious slip in the back door of our consciousness. So, while we may not necessarily dwell on the idea that we could, for instance, have an auto accident, the belief is there in race-mind consciousness. We accept the fact that car crashes happen. More importantly, we may even fear having an accident ourselves. Somewhere in our consciousness, we are *allowing* for the possibility. If an accident occurs, we may be surprised it happened to us, but all the while we were subconsciously affirming its potential. So, no — we did not create the accident, but we didn't *disagree* with the collective unconscious which assumes that misfortune occurs.

Until we make a determined effort to neutralize negative beliefs from our consciousness and replace them with spiritual principle, we will continue to be victimized by them. So, for example, every time you get into your car, proclaim you are divinely protected. State the Truth that since God is omnipresent, It is right where you are, surrounding your car and everyone else's with Its harmony. This will neutralize the negative programming. The darkness will disappear because you have turned on the light of Truth.

The Truth Always Shines

As you now know — because we are surrounded by a Law of Mind which operates by manifesting in our experience that which we accept as true — erroneous core beliefs can, and do, become our experience. The negative or limiting experiences or conditions in our lives that result from these core beliefs are somewhat illusory. They are real because they are experiential, but they're not *Reality* with a capital *"R."* Negative and limiting experiences are similar to clouds which have obscured the sun. On a cloudy day when the sun refuses to shine it's difficult to remember that indeed the sun is still shinning *behind* the clouds.

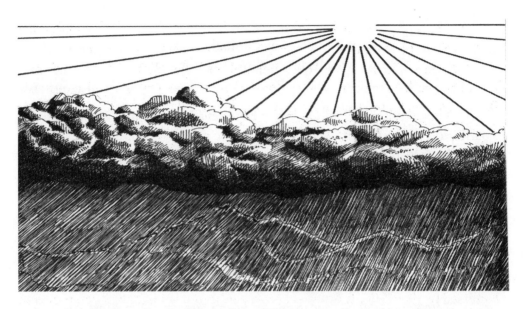

Remember, the qualities of the Universe are love, joy, peace, harmony, creativity, beauty, wholeness, perfection and abundance of good. This is Reality. When you accept without question the erroneous core beliefs of the collective unconscious, you are placing a cloud in front of the sun. Negative or limited experiences exists in front of, and obscure the Reality behind it. Negative experiences exist only because *you give them the power of your belief.* Don't forget, you have free will, being a co-creator with the Infinite. You can either choose to stand in the light of Truth, or you can choose to remain in the shadows and argue for your limitations.

"To view limitation is to impress it upon the mind," Ernest Holmes tells us in *The Science of Mind* textbook. Why? If we continue to "view limitation," our mind affirms the appearance as a solid reality. We're silently agreeing, "Yes, that's right, I *am* sick, or, I *am* broke, or, I *am* struggling, or, I *am* unhappy." We are confirming that our experience of limitation is *who we are.* We may even begin to look for evidence in our world to support the limitation. We cite unemployment figures, statistics, or someone else's experience for verification. Hence, an erroneous core belief is reinforced. Our core beliefs will continue to perpetuate themselves as experiences in our lives until we're willing to consider a different perspective.

When we let go of the limitation, we free ourselves
to create a reality of limitless good!

Think about it: Could God ever experience lack, limitation, discord, or imperfection? It could not. The Universe is the antithesis of this. It has already been established that God is all there is. And, it has already been established that what you are is God in expression. Therefore, lack, limitation, discord or imperfection cannot possibly be the Reality of you! With this understanding, you are able to see the appearance for what it is — the natural result, or manifestation, of erroneous core beliefs.

In her work, New Thought leader, Emma Curtis Hopkins describes using denial to reveal the underlying Reality behind negative appearances:

"Remember, denials mean rejecting the appearance against Good. Appearances against Good are the negative of Good. This we meet by denying the [limitation] and proclaiming the Good. It is as if something denied the Good. We meet the lie with the Truth. We meet the appearance with reality. We meet the claim of absence with the truth of presence."

We deny our good all the time. We live in a Universe which is abundant, joyous, loving, creative, intelligent, magnificent and perfect, and yet we live our lives as if these qualities had nothing to do with us. We were created by a loving presence which desires only our good, yet we refuse to accept it. We surrender to lack, limitation, sickness, unhappiness and loneliness because that's what we agree is "reality." We must stop denying our good and begin to deny "appearances against good."

EXERCISE: *Identifying Erroneous Core Beliefs*

If you have any area in your life in which the same type of problem repeats time and again (and most of us do), this a good indication that you're harboring erroneous core beliefs in that area. In the following exercise you will examine these areas and begin the process of eliminating the erroneous core beliefs that have been creating the problems.

🕑 Give yourself 10 minutes to complete this exercise.

1. Study the list below and check the boxes that correspond to areas in your life which are frequently problematic.

❏ Career	❏ Monetary supply
❏ Family relationships	❏ Friendships
❏ Committed Relationships	❏ Work relationships
❏ Feelings of inferiority	❏ Feelings of superiority
❏ Indecisiveness	❏ Lack of direction or focus
❏ Fear	❏ Unhappiness/depression
❏ Physical health	❏ Physical image
❏ Personal security	❏ Living environment
❏ Business	❏ Community/Government

2. Now close your eyes and contemplate the area or areas you have indicated. Ask your inner wisdom to shine its brilliant white light of Truth throughout your consciousness. Visualize this white light shining into every nook and cranny of your consciousness. See it light up all the dark pockets. Let this light shine upon every core belief.

3. Ask your inner wisdom to bring to the surface anything that needs healing. Ask it to show you what you need to know. "What core beliefs do I have that may be limiting my good? What beliefs have I been assuming were facts, but are really merely perceptions? Where do I have trouble knowing the Truth about myself?"

4. Open your eyes and use the space provided to jot down any ideas that may have come to you.

_____

_____

_____

_____

_____

Examining Our Attitudes

Another way of discovering our core beliefs is to examine the attitudes or *feelings* we have about certain situations. Often, this is where our core beliefs are reflected. The following are examples of some common human *attitudes* and the limiting *core beliefs* which may be reflected in them. After the core belief is revealed, a statement of Authentic Truth is offered. The next step in correcting erroneous core beliefs will be to program our consciousness with *authentic truth*.

Attitude: *"Look at the rude guy driving that expensive car. Does he think he owns the entire road? Who does he think he is? Why can't I have a cool car like that? I'll bet he cheats people to make his money."*

Possible Core Beliefs: The Universe isn't fair because it makes it easy for some to get what they want and tough for me. Rich people are rude. You have to be ruthless to make money. Therefore, I'll never get what I want unless I compromise my values.

Authentic Truth: My true nature is limitless abundance, therefore I cannot possibly be limited in any way. Everyone, including myself, has been gifted with *all* the qualities of the Universe. If one individual has abundance, then it is an affirmation that the Principle works. If this individual can manifest a beautiful car, then so can I. The same Principle that brought it to him will bring it to me. Therefore, I can be happy for this person. Also, I know that many people make money doing worthwhile things. If they can do it, so can I! Finally, it is not necessary for me to judge others.

Attitude: *"I haven't had a date in months. There are too few available men/women. I've been hurt so many times, if I did meet someone, they would probably betray me, desert me, be cruel to me or break my heart. I'll probably never meet the right person. All men/women are jerks!"*

Possible Core Belief: I'm not lovable. I don't deserve love. I deserve to be alone.

Authentic Truth: I am an expression of Love itself and I deserve all the good that God has, in fact, already given to me. This includes romantic love. I am a loving and giving person. There is a perfect partner for me to whom I can express my love and who will reciprocate. I deserve this love and I am attracting it into my life now!

Attitude: *"I hate this job. They don't appreciate me. I work too hard — and for what? I'm too talented/smart for this. I'm bored, but I can't leave because I need the insurance, got to pay my bills, need the steady paycheck, etc. Also, the economy is so bad right now, no one is hiring."*

Possible Core Belief: The Universe is limited. I'm not being taken care of. There's too much competition. Doing what I love doesn't pay the bills. I'm too old, didn't get the right education, didn't follow the correct career path, am not smart enough, not motivated enough, etc., etc. I don't have what it takes to succeed.

Authentic Truth: The limitless abundance of the Universe within me is *the* source of all my supply, not a job or anything "out there." I was created as a magnificent, intelligent and talented individual with a unique gift to give this world. It is natural for me to be fulfilled, satisfied, successful and happy in my expression. Struggle is unnecessary. I am open, and am being guided, to new opportunities which are unfolding in my life right now. The Universe supports me with an all-sufficiency as I "abound to every good work."

Attitude: *"I'm always in pain because of this darn arthritis! My mother had it, now I've got it. There's nothing I can do about it. It's only going to get worse. I might as well get used to it. I guess I'm doomed to suffer."*

Possible Core Belief: I am my body. I'm frail. I'm vulnerable to disease, genetics and aging. My body is defective. There is no mercy.

Authentic Truth: I am pure Spirit temporarily housed in a body that is not solid matter. My body is a collection of swirling energy and Intelligence — Divine Intelligence — which knows only wholeness and perfection. Therefore, every single cell and function of my body is, in essence, whole and perfect. It has been only my *belief* that has made it appear otherwise. The spiritual prototype of wholeness and perfection is now being restored. My suffering is not ordained. There is a solution to this pain and I am being guided to it.

Our attitudes can give us clues to the beliefs we have about ourselves and the world. In particular, attitudes that are accompanied by emotion are significant signals that our thinking may be misguided. Our emotions are red flags waving us in the direction of our core beliefs. Therefore, if we pay attention, emotions can serve us well.

Focus On What Is Working

Although all of us have areas in our lives that could use improvement, most of us have mastered at least one area. For example, some people have a repeating pattern of pain and failure in their relationships, but are successful in their careers and have manifested an abundance of money. For others, money may be tight or their career is not happening, but loving relationships come naturally. Some have health challenges, yet they have plenty of money or a loving family. Have you ever noticed how most people seem to focus on (if not obsess about) that one painful area, instead of what is going well? The point is, give yourself credit for whichever area of your life works and be thankful that it flows as it should. It is a law of the Universe that whatever we give our attention to, grows. Therefore, focus on, and give thanks for, *the good*. In the areas that aren't working, you are simply housing, and perhaps *nursing,* negative core beliefs.

Please remember, this is not a blame game. Resist the urge to blame yourself for creating negative experiences in your life. If you catch yourself saying "If only I'd had the correct belief system, none of this would have happened" or "If only my parents hadn't installed this poverty consciousness in me," nip such thoughts in the bud. Blaming yourself or others for things you, or they, could not possibly have known, does not serve anyone. Each of us is in the process of learning. Some learn consciously while others do it the hard way. Either way, learning and growing is the most rewarding part of life!

Few human beings have achieved master status. Those who are a few steps ahead have, most likely, been working on it longer. So*, be gentle and patient with yourself.* This is a *process* and may take some time and effort. Core beliefs are often deeply rooted and need regular weeding. They do not need to be obsessed about, or even given much attention to, but they do need to be weeded. *Pull the weeds, then focus on the roses.*

Analogy:

You've decided to plant roses in your garden. The first thing you must do is clear the soil of all rocks, weeds and debris. After the ground is prepared, you plant your rose cuttings. The next week while watering your new plants, you notice that the weeds you pulled are growing back. Does this stop you? Do you throw up your hands and say, "Well, I guess I'll never have roses, because look at all these weeds!"? Of course not. You pull out the weeds, confident your roses can now grow. The following week, however, you notice new weeds have replaced the old ones. Perhaps a little frustrated, you pull them out again. Next week the same thing happens. It seems the weeds are growing in as fast as you can pull them out. You finally come to accept that weeding your garden will be a constant process if you want to have beautiful roses!

Authentic Truth Affirmations

After you've examined and begun to uproot limiting core beliefs, the next step is to replace them with Authentic Truth Affirmations. Affirmations can be a very effective tool, but only *after* you've recognized your erroneous core beliefs and have begun to weed them. Those who do not have success with affirmations have not yet dealt with the underlying core belief. You, however, have already accomplished this with the exercises and processes in the preceding section as well as in the previous chapter. *Now,* properly structured affirmations will serve you well.

Affirmations are a series of short sentences that state the Truth about you. They remind you that, contrary to the voice of the false self, you are a unique expression of the allness of Spirit and the Kingdom of Heaven is yours now. Through the process of repeating affirmations, you remember that Universal God is all there is, that God is good, and that this Power is in every area of your life *right now.*

Affirmations correct the lies of the false self. They also erect an imaginary gate in our minds, shutting out the erroneous perceptions of the collective unconscious. The truth is, we are repeating affirmations all the time — however, most affirm our *lack* of good. If you listen close enough, you may catch your false self affirming "The odds are against me," "I'm not good enough," "I can't do it," "I'm too old," "That's just my luck" or "Don't get your hopes up." These negative affirmations will remain outside that imaginary barrier if we reinforce the gate with authentic truth affirmations.

The purpose of affirmations is not to deny an *experience* of limitation or discord. They are for the purpose of *correcting the belief that this experience is who you are.* Contrary to popular belief, your experience in not your identity. When you state the authentic truth about yourself, *in the present tense*, you are affirming that you are as the Infinite created you.

Troward explains the importance of stating the authentic truth about ourselves in the present tense, regardless of appearances to the contrary.

> "To do this is to work upon the plane of the *absolute*, and for this purpose we must endeavour to impress upon our subjective mind the idea of that which we desire quite apart from any condition. This separation from the elements of condition implies the elimination of the idea of time, and consequently we must think of the thing as already in actual existence."

No condition has altered your essential nature. Affirm the absolute Truth about yourself and you will observe it blossom into manifestation.

Examples of Authentic Truth Affirmations:

◆ **Love and Joy:** Universal Love and Joy finds an outlet of expression through me. In fact, there is no place where Spirit leaves off and I begin. Therefore, all that God is, I am — and all that It has, is mine. I am Love in expression. I am Joy in expression.

◆ **Peace and Confidence:** The Universe is not complete without me. I am essential. I am the beloved. I remain as the Infinite created me, whole, complete and perfect. I am centered in peace and joy at all times. I radiate confidence and enthusiasm.

◆ **Prosperity:** Because I am an individualized expression of the Infinite Unbounded, I am a prosperous being. I am supplied from the Infinite Source with unlimited abundance. I prosper in everything I do. I know that I exist in limitless possibility and Infinite Good is right where I am and active in my experience.

◆ **Health:** I did not create my body. Original Perfect Substance became the form of my body which Spirit now uses to express Itself. My body is therefore inherently perfect. Divine Intelligence infuses every cell and function of my body and sustains it now. All seeming illness is only manifested false beliefs which I let go of now. Perfect Intelligence, expressing as my body, is completely restored.

◆ **Relationships:** I know there is a Divine Presence within me and within everyone. Each being is a unique incarnation of Spirit. Because I am aware of this Divine Presence it responds to me. The authentic self within me reaches out and communes with the authentic self in every individual. I express love fully and everyone expresses their love fully to me.

Feel free to copy and use the affirmations listed here that relate to your concerns. In addition, the *"Authentic Truth"* listed under the core belief examples can be used as affirmations. Or better still, use the exercise below to write your own personalized affirmations. Carry them with you wherever you go and read them frequently. Tack them up in your home or office. Tape them to the mirror in your bathroom. Repeat them as often as possible throughout the day whenever you hear the negative voice of the false self. *Frequency is key.*

EXERCISE: *Core Belief Shift*

1. Select three of the "problematic areas" which you discovered in the first exercise (*Identifying Erroneous Core Beliefs*.) Focus on one area at a time. In the space provided under "Core Beliefs" jot down the belief which you feel has contributed to the blockage of good in that area.

2. Next, create an authentic truth affirmation for neutralizing the false core belief. Study the sample affirmations as well as the "authentic truth" corrections in the preceding section. Notice they all begin with a unifying theme,

which is: "I am one with the Infinite," then proceeds to affirm the truth about yourself in regards to a particular condition. This is the structure of an authentic truth affirmation. The affirmation you create should cause you to remember the Truth about yourself and the particular situation or condition for which you're treating. Remember, the *appearance* of limitation has temporarily obscured Reality, your affirmation is now *revealing* the Truth.

1a) Core Belief:

_____

_____

_____

_____

1b) Authentic Truth Affirmation:

_____

_____

_____

_____

2a) Core Belief:

_____

_____

_____

2b) Authentic Truth Affirmation:

_____

_____

_____

_____

3a) Core Belief:

_____

_____

_____

_____

3b) Authentic Truth Affirmation:

_____

_____

_____

_____

Get into the habit of listening to your thoughts. Take your mind off "auto-pilot" and take back the controls. When you hear limiting thoughts, get out your mental eraser. Then, immediately replace that thought with an authentic truth affirmation.

Remember *you* have dominion over the core beliefs that occupy your mind and *you* have the power to change them! Stay with the process, weed constantly, practice your affirmations frequently and work to apply these Principles to your life. In doing so, you will break free from the bonds of apparent limitation and open the door for miracles to occur.

CHAPTER SEVEN

THE LAW OF ATTRACTION

"Like attracts like and it is also true that we may become attracted to something which is greater than our previous experience by first embodying the atmosphere of our desires."
— *Ernest Holmes*

We live in an orderly Universe which is governed by definite *spiritual* principles or laws to the same degree that it is governed by *physical* principles or laws. We are subject to all physical laws until we appreciate how they operate and understand how to utilize them; then they become available for our use. In exactly the same way, we are subject to spiritual principles or laws until we appreciate how they operate and understand how to utilize them; then they become available for our use. One of these principles is the Law of Attraction, which is as real as any physical law. Just as we now utilize the law of aerodynamics, we will be able to utilize the law of attraction for our purposes when we understand how it works. Until we do, *we* are subject to *it*. In fact, we are using the law of attraction all the time, however, without our awareness — thus unknowingly attracting lack, limitation, chaos, failure and unhappiness. When we learn to use this law properly, we will be able to attract the love, prosperity, success, fulfillment and peace we desire.

Each of us is surrounded by an atmosphere of our thinking. More to the point, *we* exist within *it*. Similar to a plastic figure that exists within the bubble of his snow globe, we exist within the bubble of our "thought atmosphere." In the Absolute, we live, move and have our being in God. In the relative (our human experience) we live, move and have our being within our own thought atmosphere.

This thought atmosphere is the sum total of our *inner subjective understanding* which contains the following:

- Core beliefs which originate from the erroneous perceptions of the false self (i.e., "I am separate from my good, I am inadequate").

- Core beliefs which originate from our authentic self ("I am talented, capable, lovable," etc.).

- Core beliefs which originate from the collective unconscious ("life is a struggle").

- Resentments and lack of forgiveness toward ourselves and others.

- Our capacity to love and give to others.

- Our reaction to events and circumstances.

The combination of the above elements creates an overall representation in our thought atmosphere which acts as a magnet, attracting to us, or repelling from us, people, experiences, situations and conditions. Rather than an individual thought or belief, it is our overall subjective understanding that is responsible for creating our world. It is the content of our internal thought atmosphere that manifests as analogous external experience. One is the invisible essence, the other is the manifest form. Perhaps it was this understanding that prompted 17th Century philosopher Baruch Spinoza to proclaimed, "I do not say that mind is one thing and matter is another, I say they are the same thing."

In *The Science of Mind*, Ernest Holmes gives us a key for utilizing the Law of Attraction:

> "This mental atmosphere is the direct result of [one's] conscious and unconscious thought, which in its turn, becomes the direct reason for, and cause of, that which comes into [one's] life. Through this power we are either attracting or repelling. Like attracts like and it is also true that we may become attracted to something which is greater than our previous experience by first embodying the atmosphere of our desire."

The key to changing our current thought atmosphere (thereby attracting to us what we desire) is to first *embody the atmosphere of our desire.* We have the ability to create a thought atmosphere that will irresistibly attract success, love, prosperity, vibrant health, peace, joy, fulfillment or whatever our heart desires.

Thought Atmosphere Dynamics

We'll use Ben to illustrate how this principle works. Ben has difficulty accepting the idea that he is prosperous when he's being paid a modest salary, there are pay increase ceilings at his company, and he has an extraordinary amount of bills which include his mother's medical care. He is, in effect, going deeper into debt every month. These are the "facts" of his life as it stands right now. Historically, Ben has always lived financially close to the edge and it looks like things are getting worse. Accepting the "truth" that he is prosperous seems like a lie to Ben.

Jesus told us to "judge not according to appearances." He did not say appearances were not genuine; he was telling us not to accept them as Reality, not to be hypnotized by them. Even though Ben's facts appear irrefutable, they are still, in essence, *appearances.* These appearances are a direct reflection of his thought atmosphere. Several elements have combined to create and reinforce Ben's thought atmosphere of limitation: For instance, his false-self core beliefs ("I am separate from my good"), his fearful reaction to the experience of limitation, his acceptance of the collective unconscious' core beliefs ("Not enough good to go around"), and some resentment towards his mother for not setting up a proper savings plan — all of which are on a subconscious level. This thought atmosphere has, in turn, been attracting increasing experiences of limitation in his life. In essence, Ben has been giving his power away to a set of circumstances and he will continue to be a victim of them until he changes his thought atmosphere — *until he rises above the appearances.* He must lift up his vision to see the Reality of Infinite good and realize that he is an inseparable part of this Reality.

Whenever we look to our good as being "out there" somewhere, we are looking at an *effect.* And, all effects are inherently limited. If we think our income is generated by our employer, our spouse, our investments, or our sales commissions, then we are looking to the *effects* for our *source*. Our employer, spouse, investments or sales commissions are simply the *vehicles* in which our abundance is channeled to us. They are not the source. Our source is the Infinite limitless abundance of the Universe — and *it is within us*. Indeed, this is the source of all our good, whether it be our life, our breath, our love, our joy, our peace, our ideas, our creativity, or our monetary supply. Our job or investments are simply the *conduits* through which the Universe *channels* money to us. Limitless Invisible Substance is *the* Source of all manifest form and it is *boundless*. When we open up to the idea that this Substance exists within us now, we vibrate with the awareness that we *have* abundance; *that energetic attracts to us the physical form of prosperity*. The Universe is now free to find new and expanded avenues to channel prosperity to us.

"Beloved, I wish above all things that thou mayest prosper." *(3Jn2)*

Let's say Ben begins to understand this basic principle. Following are exercises Ben could do to change his thought atmosphere to attract boundless abundance into his life. If you are experiencing any form of lack, please follow along with Ben.

EXERCISE: *Changing Thought Atmosphere*

Step 1: *Get it out on paper*

Take out a separate sheet of paper and on the first line write: <u>What is preventing me from experiencing prosperity?</u> Next, list all the reasons why you are experiencing limitation. Get it out of your head and on to paper. Don't be afraid to give words to these thoughts; they do you no good hiding in your subconscious mind. Is the reason you're experiencing financial problems because your boss doesn't pay you enough?; because you don't have an advanced degree and can't get a higher paying job?; because your mother's medical bills are exorbitant?; because your line of work historically pays low?; because you're lazy?; because you can't get that rich girl to marry you? List all the reasons you think might be the cause of your financial lack.

Now write at the top of the paper in large, bold letters the words: EF-FECTS / APPEARANCES.

Step 2: *Contemplate the abundance*

Abundance is all around you. For example, examine the leaves on your favorite tree. How about the jars of spices in your pantry, or the stack of catalogues you get in the mail every week? You might have an abundance of names in your address book, or pennies in a drawer. Abundance may take the form of a collection: stamps, antique jewelry, spools of thread, magazines, tools, etc. Look around you. Take a walk in the park and consider the millions of blades of grass. Is there a pond there? Consider how many drops of water are in that pond. How many square miles of sky are there in Earth's atmosphere? How about the billions of molecules in your own body! These examples are *symbols* of the principle of abundance in action. Observe the abundance in your world and begin to *own it*. This is the domain in which you live and are an integral part of.

Step 3: *Allow this abundance to flow through you*

Sit down, relax and get comfortable. Take a nice deep breath in, hold it for a moment, then let it out. Repeat the breath two or three times. Now contemplate the invisible Substance that exists behind all the abundance in the world. This unseen Substance *expresses as* the billions of molecules in your body, the billions of stars in the heavens, the billions of leaves on all the trees. Now imagine being surrounded by a bubble which extends out three feet in every direction from your body. Imagine this same invisible Substance filling up and occupying every square inch of space within this bubble. You are totally surrounded by this loving, infinite, invisible abundance. You cannot go anywhere without this Substance going with you. Now, take a large breath and breathe in this invisible abundance. It is filling your very being with its presence. Each breath you take, you are breathing in limitless abundance of good. Every breath you breathe out, you are pouring this abundant Substance into your world. In fact, this Substance is the very breath you breathe, it is the life force which sustains you. It is a part of you and you are a part of it. It is permeating your being and radiating out from you. It is a magnetic force attracting forms and experiences of limitless prosperity into your life. This presence steadily fills your mind with creative, innovative ideas. Everywhere you go, this magnetic force of Infinite Substance, which infuses your thought atmosphere, is attracting forms and experiences of financial prosperity. Close your eyes and take a few moments to bathe in this infinite prosperity which fills your being, surrounds you and radiates out from you.

Step 4: *You have the Power*

Take another look at the list you created in step one. Notice that the "facts" you listed are really nothing but appearances. Notice that they have no inherent power over you. *You* have power over all the appearances. You understand, and have experienced, a greater truth now. Contemplate Joel Goldsmith's inspired words:

> *"God's grace removes every obstacle from our path because the light of truth reveals that there never was power in the so-called obstacle."*

The light of Truth reveals the Reality that exists behind every so-called obstacle. Your job, investments, or sales commissions are simply the vehicles in which this invisible Substance pours its prosperity into your life. Express a sense of gratitude for the *channels* of your supply and for the truth that they are now expanding. New channels are being created in your life *right now*. This moment your consciousness is being filled with golden ideas. Your radiant, abundant thought atmosphere is now attracting a limitless flow of good. Now tear up the list you wrote while repeating: *"I have the power over any circumstance. I am an individualized expression of Infinite abundance."*

Eric Butterworth tells us in *Spiritual Economics*:

104

"The secret of achieving prosperity lies in so vividly keeping yourself centered in the inner focus of affluence that you literally exude the consciousness of it. This is often called the 'prosperity consciousness.' It is not something you gain through repeating prosperity affirmations over and over. It is getting yourself centered at the root of reality within. You see abundance, not dollar signs, not things, not pots of gold at the end of a rainbow. For the rainbow is seeing the storm through the raindrops. You see the appearance of whatever the need may be through the awareness of substance. You become a purveyor of the prosperity flow."

You can also do the above exercise to attract anything you truly desire, replacing the words "abundance and prosperity" with those that represent the qualities you want to embody.

♦ For attracting love, visualize your thought atmosphere infused with limitless love which is permeating your being and radiating out from you. Feel yourself becoming irresistibly attractive to loving, like-minded individuals.

♦ For success, see the words "success," "accomplishment" and "yes" filling your thought atmosphere. Observe your mind as it is being filled with an abundance of innovative ideas. You are God's living enterprise, therefore you are already a success. Allow this joyous success to radiate out from you. Feel yourself attracting the perfect, right opportunities.

♦ For health and vitality, visualize your thought atmosphere infused with wellness, energy and perfection. Feel this presence saturate every pore, every organ, every function and every cell of your body. Feel yourself attracting supportive friends and joyous, healthful experiences.

♦ For peace and serenity, visualize your thought atmosphere infused with a peace that passeth all understanding. Breathe in and feel the waves of peace permeate your soul and radiate out from you. Feel yourself attracting peaceful and harmonious experiences.

Practice Steps 2 and 3 of the above exercise as often as you are able. It is highly effective to do the exercise in bed, right before falling off to sleep. This method will allow the ideas and feelings to slip directly into your subconscious mind. This process is very powerful. Be prepared for transformation. Get ready for an expansion of good to manifest in your life!

Right-use-ness

When we re-train our consciousness to think with righteousness — or *right-use-ness* of the Law — transformation and healing are inevitable. Emma Curtis Hopkins offered this insight:

> "Having been trained all your life on the basis of Good being absent from you, you now begin to reason from an entirely different basis. You judge not by appearance, but by righteousness. Many [negative] conditions slip away almost instantaneously. They were built up by your false general reasoning and with these gone, they have no props."

Your good has never been "absent from you." It has always been yours in the invisible state. With the tools you now have available to you, this good can be yours in the visible, manifest form.

Throughout history, individuals have prospered regardless of poor economic conditions, including the "great depression." It *is* true that the rich get richer and the poor get poorer. Why? Because the rich have a thought atmosphere of abundance which automatically attracts an abundance of money. The poor have a thought atmosphere of poverty and struggle which automatically attracts more poverty and struggle. Even if those with this "struggle-mindset" are presented with an outstanding opportunity, they will likely sabotage it because the idea of good fortune is foreign to their system. On the other end of the spectrum, if one has a thought atmosphere filled with possibility and prosperity, no outer condition or event will be able to withhold what's theirs by divine right.

Example:

Reverend Marlene Morris of the Religious Science Church in Burbank, California inherited a home when an elder member of the congregation passed on. Her intention was to sell the home and use the proceeds to renovate the church. However, this occurred during the worst economic slump in Southern California history. Hundreds of homes were going into foreclosure every week. Many were on the market for years. Despite the circumstances, she put the home on the market for a relatively high price. Everyone thought she was crazy, including the real estate agent and prospective buyers who made offers at one third the asking price. This minister, whose thought atmosphere is consistently infused with love and abundance, stood firm. To everyone's amazement, the house sold within a few weeks for her original asking price, and she transformed that well-worn church into a thing of beauty!

First Cause

In New Thought, the Law of Attraction is sometimes referred to the Law of Cause and Effect. The beliefs in our thought atmosphere are considered *cause* while the things and experiences that our beliefs have attracted are *effects*. From a larger perspective the thoughts of Universal Intelligence are what is known as First Cause or Cause with a big "C." First Cause created the natural world which includes all beauty, abundance, love, joy and peace. First Cause is "The Absolute" and it exists within our authentic self. When we are in alignment with this self, we are in the realm of the Absolute and our thought atmosphere is automatically imbued with First Cause. When this occurs, we become unobstructed channels for Love-Intelligence to flow into every area of our life.

When we forget who we are and align with the fearful false self, we are creating our life from a limited awareness. This is cause with a small "c." Cause with a small "c" attracts the effect of limitation — or at best, only temporary satisfaction. Shifting our awareness to our authentic self, allows us to utilize First Cause, which is the Creative Power of the Universe. When we set our intention (our heart's desire) employing First Cause, we rise above circumstance and our success is assured.

Again, we turn to Troward for his keen insight:

> "It is essential to know whether we are consciously making use of first cause with a definite purpose or not, and the criterion is this: If we regard the fulfillment of our purpose as contingent upon any circumstances, past, present, or future, we are not making use of first cause; we have descended to the level of secondary causation, which is the region of doubts, fears and limitation...by forming the idea in the Absolute, and maintaining that idea, we have shaped the first cause into the desired form and can await the results with joyous expectancy."

In order to create a new effect in your life, it's necessary to create a new Cause *independent of any previous experience.* If you have experienced a history of failure in a particular area, and you now choose to create success, you must begin in the Absolute, free from the insidious grip of past experience. This is accomplished by declaring your freedom from the collective unconscious which believes there is not enough to go around, life is difficult and relationships are painful. Declare your freedom from being at the effect of circumstances. Declare your freedom from the belief that you are separate from your Source. Declare your freedom by identifying with the limitless Power which is your authentic self. This Power is not contingent upon any previous condition. This moment is *new*. Today is a new beginning. Your past cannot touch you unless you allow it. No matter what has transpired in the past, what the circumstances are at this moment, or what others say, you are a success now and nothing can hinder you from accomplishing your goal! The Universe is *for* you. From this moment on, everything is working together for your good. Understand this truth, then act as if it were so.

> "Your holiness reverses all the laws of the world. It is beyond every restriction of time, space, distance, and limits of any kind."
> —*A Course In Miracles*

Program Success

Your mind is much like a computer. The power is neutral, but *you* supply the programming. When you know *you* have the power to create new programming, you can design the life of your dreams! Practice actively deleting the negative programming that says you are subject to a world of struggle, suffering, sickness and lack. Mentally hit the "delete key!" Now mentally hit the "insert key" that programs your true nature, which is prosperous, joyously happy and fulfilled, successful, creative, healthy, loving and loved, harmonious and peaceful. The truth is that your "mental computer" doesn't care what instruction it receives. It will run any programming you give it.

Analogy:

Let's suppose you are the projectionist in a movie theater. The projector is nothing more than a machine which projects onto a screen whatever film is placed inside it. It doesn't care what kind of film it shows. Let's say you are showing a very sad movie this month. It is a very real experience for the audience, and they react by becoming depressed and teary. Then, next month you change the film you are showing to a comedy. The projector would never protest or refuse to show the new movie. It's impartial. The experience of the audience however, is very different this time.

In the same way, Energy flows from its unlimited source through your consciousness, filtered by your thought atmosphere, and projects its contents onto the screen of your life. The Energy doesn't care how you use it. It's neutral. However, your successes and failures are determined by *what film you've put into the projector.*

The Importance of Circulation

Just as important as receiving our good from the Kingdom, we need to circulate what we receive by *giving* to others. This circulation keeps the channel open and flowing. We block the flow when we hoard our good. Hoarding sends a message to the Universe that we're afraid if we give our good away, there will be none left. We need to understand that our good is inexhaustible because it comes from an Unlimited Source. Truly, the more we give, the more the Universe pours its gifts into our lives. We cannot out-give the Universe.

As an experiment, try for a week to give past the point of your comfort level. Stretch your giving muscles a little. Then simply observe as the Universe gives you twice as much of whatever you gave. This givingness can include your talents, your time, your love, or your money. You will be directed where and how you should give by asking your inner wisdom. You can give to your loved ones, your friends, strangers down on their luck, to your community as well as to the source of your spiritual support (i.e., tithing).

Whatever gift you feel moved to give, you must offer it in love, and not from any sense of obligation. If you give with expectation of return, or even acknowledgment, your gift goes forth with strings attached. In order for the Universe to give freely to you, you must give freely to others.

Our Reactions

Another important element in our thought atmosphere is the manner in which we *react* to events. If we react with anger or fear to a situation that occurs, we are binding that experience to us and inviting it to revisit us. When we're able to claim a blessing from every experience in our life, no matter how painful, then a blessing is what we'll receive. There is a lesson for us in every experience and when we learn what that lesson is, we will no longer need to repeat it. Ask your inner wisdom to reveal the lesson and the blessing in *each* experience.

Example:

I was in the process of changing careers and was employed by a well known movie studio. I was working for the Executive VP and it was a very stressful office. In addition, my boss was prone to fits of temper. He had been through several assistants, some of whom had left in tears. I was practicing spiritual principles regularly at the time, so, I decided not to take his anger personally. I knew he was under pressure and had not learned to handle it well. I silently sent him love and claimed a blessing for the experience of being there. I consciously infused my thought atmosphere with love and a sense of limitless opportunity. Before long, not only did his response to me change, but I met a man who worked in the same building who would later become my husband! In addition, I transferred to the creative development department, which opened up a more rewarding career for me.

This same principle applies to experiences of crisis and even personal tragedy. Tragedies, and events beyond our control do occur. It's how we *perceive* the event that shapes *our experience*. A tragedy can either crush us or motivate us to expand and reveal personal strengths we never knew we possessed. In Chinese the words *crisis* and *opportunity* are represented by the same symbol. Instead of asking "Why me?" we want to ask, "What can I learn from this experience?" or "How can *I* be a blessing in this situation?" If we allow it, our personal crisis may serve as an opportunity for a deeper understanding of who and what we are. In fact, it might be helpful to re-label "tragedy" or "crisis" as a "challenging experience" or an "opportunity for growth." This re-labeling re-qualifies the energy so that the experience may serve as a catalyst for our personal expansion.

Example:

My friend, Ricardo Abrines, lost his son in a tragic accident. The sudden loss of a child is probably the most horrific experience one can endure. For the next several months, Ricardo went through a normal, healthy process of grieving. But after a time, the pain of his loss was so unbearable, it forced him to re-evaluate his response. He began to embrace a sense of gratitude for the eighteen years he was blessed to have his son in his life. His persistent search to find a blessing in the tragedy uncovered a new understanding of the eternality of life. Ricardo discovered he was free from the largest fear most people have — the fear of death. But, he did not stop there — he was determined to extract something from this experience that would bless others as well. Ricardo now helps parents who are having trouble with their teenagers by sharing his story and discussing the priority of love and the precious gift of live itself.

EXERCISE: *Creating a New Cause*

You've learned from this chapter that all *effects* in life originate from the *cause* of beliefs in our thought atmosphere. The following is an exercise which will change the *cause*, thereby changing the *effects* in your life. In essence, you will be inserting a new "film" into your "mental projector" thereby playing the real-life movie you desire.

First, record a specific goal you would like to see fulfilled. It may be something you would like to accomplish, a more expanded way of expressing yourself, or a lifestyle you would like to have.

My Goal:

_____

_____

_____

Next, list three people you know (or know of) who have manifested in *their* life a similar experience that you desire in *your* life. Then, next to their names, list the individual's personal qualities or attributes. For example: are they powerful and dynamic, poised and confident, intelligent or creative? Do they seem to prosper in everything they do? Are they committed and disciplined? Are they at peace with themselves and with the world? Are they great communicators? Are they easy-going or enthusiastic? Are they loving and generous? Does everything they touch turn to gold? Make a list of all the qualities you admire in these individuals:

Person #1:	Qualities:
_____	_____
	_____
	_____
	_____
Person #2:	Qualities:
_____	_____
	_____
	_____
	_____
	_____
Person #3:	Qualities:
_____	_____
	_____
	_____
	_____

After reading the following paragraphs, close your eyes for a few moments and focus on these ideas:

- If it is true that we are individual expressions of the One, then we all possess, in equal measure, all the attributes of that One. Visualize yourself and each individual you've listed above as sunbeams existing next to each other, radiating out from the Sun. The light they shine is the exact same light that is radiating from you. The particles that make up their sunbeam are identical to those that exist in you.

- You possess the same spiritual qualities as those you admire because, in Reality, you are made of the same one Intelligence. Every one of us has been given an equal amount of life Energy to use as we choose. Therefore, any and all spiritual qualities *they* possess, *you* also possess. Embrace and embody them. In Truth, you are powerful, limitless, confident, poised, at peace, enthusiastic, intelligent, creative, focused, successful and affluent *now*. In Truth, you prosper in everything you do. You are an effective communicator. You are loved and loving. You are magnificent. Feel this in your bones. All the qualities of this One Energy have already been given to you. In fact, there is no place where this One leaves off and you begin. *All that this One is, you are right now.* Stay with this vision until it is more real to you than the current circumstances in your life. When you are ready, open your eyes.

Pick up your pencil and answer the following questions:

- Who are you? (List the qualities you've just been experiencing.)

I am:

_____

_____

_____

_____

• With this new awareness of your divine qualities, what are you able to do?

I can / I am doing:

_____

_____

_____

_____

• What is your environment? (See yourself in a specific place doing what you love to do, or expressing the way you've always wanted.)

I am in:

_____

_____

_____

_____

• Now that you are expressing your potential, how do you affect others? (Do you inspire others and in what way? Do others seek your opinion, etc.?)

I affect others by:

_____

_____

_____

_____

Congratulations! You have created a new cause — which is now in the process of becoming a new effect in your life. To reinforce this new reality, read what you have written here every day for the next few weeks. Spend some time each day contemplating the truth about yourself, incorporating these new ideas into your thought atmosphere. Then, simply "await the results with joyous expectancy."

CHAPTER EIGHT

THE POWER OF FORGIVENESS

"When you meet anyone, remember it is a holy encounter. As you see him you will see yourself. As you treat him you will treat yourself. As you think of him, you will think of yourself. Never forget this, for in him you will find yourself or lose yourself."
—A Course In Miracles

In addition to our core beliefs, the influence of the collective unconsciousness, and the manner in which we react to events, there is another element that carries a great deal of weight in our thought atmosphere, and therefore in our experience — it is our ability, or inability, to forgive. Whenever we harbor resentment toward people or situations, or fail to forgive ourselves, we are creating a very real blockage in our energy which keeps us stuck in life. A thought atmosphere filled with resentment attracts to the individual repeated relational difficulties, as well as problems in other areas of life that may appear unrelated.

We may set our intention in the fertile soil of creative mind, shift our core beliefs from lack to limitless good, and water our garden with authentic truth affirmations, but if we are unwilling to forgive anything or anyone, the weeds of resentment will choke off the flow of our good. The only way a new experience of good can find a place to express through us, is if we clear the channel of those attitudes which are not constructive. Manifesting prosperity, success, health and love on a permanent basis requires a consciousness free of judgment and blame. Therefore, our work is not complete until we let go of each and every resentment.

Forgiveness is the key that opens the door to personal freedom. Forgiving ourselves for our own transgressions, and forgiving those who have transgressed against us frees us to realize our potential. Believe me, I realize that this is oftentimes much easier said than done! Forgiveness may be a difficult lesson, but it is essential for our growth and ultimate happiness.

Example:

My dear friend Rhonda Britten had a tragedy occur in her life — a tragedy not many can imagine. When she was 14 years old, she witnessed her father shooting and killing her mother, then shooting and killing himself. In less than 5 minutes, this man had taken away the most important thing in a young child's life and left an indelible impression of violence and horror upon her developing psyche. Because she was a religious girl, she knew the only Christian thing to do was to forgive her Dad — which she did to the best of her ability. Only later did she discover her act of forgiving was, understandably, superficial at best.

Her difficulties adjusting to life alone, tormented by anger and fear began to manifest in her early twenties. She would frequently act out by drinking and manipulating men. Unable to sleep, she became anxious, depressed and hopeless. Rhonda's pain became so unbearable she attempted suicide three times. Finally, at the age of twenty-seven Rhonda decided if she were to make it in life, she would have to sincerely forgive her father, not just give lip service to it.

As she achieved deeper and more meaningful levels of love and forgiveness, she began to open to her own inner peace as well as life's possibilities. Her fear subsided as she learned to trust that she was safe in God's universe. Her spirituality deepened with each passing day. Now, as a Professional Life & Career Coach and licensed Religious Science Practitioner, Rhonda assists others in living successful lives.

Could anyone blame Rhonda for hating her father for his horrendous crime? Most of us would think she was justified in harboring enormous resentment toward him *forever.* However, if she had chosen that path, she would have continued to be a victim, leading a life of self-abuse and dysfunction. Also, she never would have realized the tremendous healing and blessing which was in store for her, not to mention the blessings for those she now assists. Within our ability to forgive lies the power to completely transform our lives, opening up the floodgates for untold blessings to occur.

Fortunately, most of us do not have as challenging a lesson in forgiveness as my friend. For the majority of us, forgiving someone who has broken our heart or cheated us in a business deal seems like a distasteful, if not impossible, task. Many times it's more difficult for us to forgive *those we love* because we tend to hold them at a higher standard. *The key to being able to forgive anyone is to separate who they really are from what they've done, and behold their authentic self.*

When we forgive others we are not condoning their behavior. And, it doesn't mean we have to invite them over for dinner either! Forgiveness doesn't mean excusing what someone has done. It is admitting that the individual is a fallible human being who has temporarily forgotten who he or she is. What forgiveness does is free *us* from the heavy burden of resentment. If we can separate what someone has done in the past from who they are, let go of the history and begin again in this moment, we will not only be healing our lives, we

120

will also be contributing to the shift in the collective unconscious, making it easier for the world to forgive.

> Without inner peace, it is impossible to have world peace.
> —Dalai Lama

When considering the one who has hurt us, we must understand that one of two things has occurred:

1. This individual had no awareness that their actions would cause another pain. He or she was simply following their own path (however unenlightened we think it is) and we simply stepped into it. *Also,* we are taking their behavior personally.

2. This individual was unaware of his or her authentic self and allowed the fearful, false self to take over. The behavior which issued forth from their false self intentionally hurt us. Remember, the false self is the frightened and unloving shadow which is mistaken for the real person. Although not always expressed, behind this mask is the authentic self which is pure love. If this person knew the love which existed inside them, and were able to express it, they would have done so.

As human beings, we are naturally flawed. We all make mistakes. In some faiths this is interpreted as "original sin," and one who continues to sin is known as a "sinner." The word "sin" is actually of Greek origin. It was used in archery and referred to "missing the mark." Missing the mark is not a sin — it's a mistake. A person who makes a mistake is not called a "mistaker." He or she is just someone who has made a mistake.

The whole idea of sin has been grotesquely transformed to imply that someone who makes mistakes is bad and doesn't deserve our forgiveness — that only God can forgive a sinner. We need to understand that no one is inherently bad. All of us are born innocent, and as we make our way through life, we forget who we are and therefore make mistakes. Some, because of upbringing, or lack of self-esteem, might act in a way that we perceive as bad and impossible to forgive. It *is* possible to forgive *anyone* if we separate the authentic person from

121

his or her mistakes. Ignorance of one's connection to God produces fear and lack of self-esteem which are generally the unconscious motivating factors behind all destructive behavior. Therefore, *all we ever need to forgive is ignorance.*

Have you ever noticed that when you're holding a grudge against someone, they continue to be a problem in your life? What feelings are brought up when you think about them? Do you feel rising anger, a sinking heart, frustration, fear? Even when you are not actively thinking about this person or situation, the anger is still there, buried in your cellular memory. Practitioners of mind/body medicine tell us that many illnesses are caused by an unforgiving attitude. Even those in traditional medicine have proven that our emotions do play an important role in our health. It's about time they noticed. The truth is, bitterness and rancor are toxins which poison the body temple.

We must also remember that our unwillingness to forgive never affects the individual who hurt us. Of course not. It only harms *us.* When we perceive that someone has wronged us, we allow a wound to develop within us which festers over time as we continue to nurse it with resentment. This wound hinders our ability to become whole, which in turn, adversely affects other areas of our lives. Forgiveness heals and releases us from a poisoned body and an unfulfilled life. Reverend Morrissey tells us in her book, *Building Your Field of Dreams*:

> "Those emotions create a tremendous void in us and around us. If you refuse to forgive, all those toxic feelings of hatred and resentment stay bottled up inside, eventually seeping into other areas of your life. The offender doesn't suffer. It is your own life, your own dreams that are stunted...In order to free the dream inside you, practice forgiveness every day."

Our willingness to forgive heals all wounds and releases the natural free flow of good to pour into our lives. The following passage from *A Course In Miracles* eloquently describes the power of forgiveness:

> "Ask not to be forgiven, for this has already been accomplished. Ask rather to learn how to forgive. Forgive the world and you will understand that everything that God created cannot have an end and

nothing he did not create is real. Do you want peace? Forgiveness offers it. Do you want happiness, a quiet mind, a certainty of purpose and a sense of worth and beauty that transcends the world? Do you want care and safety and the warmth of sure protection always? Do you want a quietness that cannot be disturbed, a gentleness that never can be hurt, a deep abiding comfort and a rest so perfect it can never be upset? All this forgiveness offers you.

You who want peace can find it only by complete forgiveness. Forgive the past and let it go, for it is gone. Lift up your eyes and look on one another in innocence born of complete forgiveness of each other's illusions. Whom you forgive is given power to forgive you your illusions. By your gift of freedom is it given unto you. Those who forgive are thus releasing themselves from illusion, while those who withhold forgiveness are binding themselves to them."

Also, after you have sincerely forgiven someone, your relationship with them will be recreated; they'll change, you'll change, the dynamic of the relationship will change, they may disappear altogether from your life, or you will no longer be affected by them. In short, you will be free. *And*, a large blessing will be in store for you.

The same principle applies to those who have either passed away, or are no longer in our lives, but who still have an effect on us. A friend once said, "My mother is always criticizing me...and she's been dead for 10 years." Until we forgive others we will be victims, shackled by the chains they've tied around us. Let's give *ourselves* a break. *We* hold the key to personal empowerment — and that is through forgiveness.

Forgiving When It's Difficult

Although it may be more difficult to forgive someone who has committed a violent crime; in the case of my friend, it is possible and ultimately necessary to be able to transcend the painful experience. This doesn't mean we should not first own and be able to express our anger. Getting in touch with our true feelings is an essential step. In fact, sometimes anger can be constructive. For example, Candy Lightner effectively channeled her anger over losing her child by founding the organization, MADD (Mothers Against Drunk Drivers) which helps save the lives of others.

In the exercise at the end of the chapter we will briefly explore the process of releasing emotions, including anger. However, for a deeper processing of anger, joining a support group is highly recommended. If there's not one in your town, connect with a therapist and start a group together. After the process of releasing the anger has been completed, we must learn to finally let go and embrace forgiveness.

Forgiveness is, many times, a process that begins with only a *willingness* to forgive. This is where forgiveness starts. Complete forgiveness is a goal we move closer to each time we practice. Keep in mind that when we for*give* someone, we are actually giving a gift to ourselves. Our willingness to forgive opens the channels within us to allow the gifts of peace, joy, healing and the manifestation of our dreams to pour into our lives.

Forgiveness As a Way of Life

When the 60s generation looked around at society's institutions and the corporate world they observed a phenomenon occurring which they did not want to repeat. The prevalent attitude within society was "I'm looking out for number one!" and "The end (bottom line, profit) justifies *any* means." The younger generation was instrumental in opening a dialogue about ethical business practices and about what really contributes to a person's happiness. Then came the 80s and we fell back asleep. Many a 60s "hippie" became seduced by the intoxicating aroma of a quick rise to wealth and power, refusing to look at who might be paying the price.

While it appears that self-interested people often get what they want, what is more likely is that, soon after someone gets what he or she wants (particularly if at someone else's expense) such a gain only creates more emptiness. Thus begins the vicious circle of the false self acquiring more, yet feeling less satisfied. Also, those who are always looking after "number one" usually create more problems that need looking after.

"Nobody can benefit us; nobody can harm us. It is what goes out from us that returns to bless or to condemn us. We create our own good and we create our own evil."

—*Joel Goldsmith*

Since we are, on an essential level, all one, then *what we do to others, we are doing to ourselves — literally, not figuratively*. This is the law of karma, or as we chanted in the 60s: "What goes around, comes around." Pretend as we might, we cannot hide from a spiritual law. For our own sake, it's time we remembered this fundamental Truth. If we treat others with disrespect, we will be treated reciprocally. If we cheat others, we will be cheated. If we lie to others, others will lie to us. If we judge and condemn others, we are inviting judgment and condemnation from others. Whatever we do to others will be done unto us; not necessarily by that individual, but the deed will revisit us somewhere down the line.

If people are lying to us, cheating us or treating us badly, we must examine the way we've treated others. Even if we *silently* resent others, we are broadcasting negative energy into the Universe and it will, most assuredly, come back to us.

The only way off this karmic wheel is through *forgiveness — of ourselves and others*. We are all spiritually connected — and we can no longer assume that our actions do not affect others. When seen in this light, forgiveness becomes a method for breaking down the barriers between "self" and "other" — for truly there is no separation. When we come to this realization we will naturally want to treat others as we would like to be treated, because *they are us*. We will then *automatically* live in integrity with one of the greatest spiritual laws in the Universe.

It's no coincidence that every major religion has its own version of the *Golden Rule:*

Christianity: "Do unto others as you would have them do unto you."

Islam: "No one of you is a believer until he loves for his brother what he loves for himself."

Taoism: "Regard your neighbor's gain as your own gain and regard your neighbor's loss as your own loss."

Judaism:	"Thou shalt love thy neighbor as thyself."
Hinduism:	"Men gifted with intelligence should always treat others as they wish to be treated."
Sikhism:	"As Thou deemest thyself so deem others. Then shalt thou become a partner in heaven."
Buddhism:	"In five ways should a clansman minister to his friends and familiars — by generosity, courtesy and benevolence, by treating them as he treats himself, and by being as good as his word."

The Golden Rule is a common thread in every major religion because it is a Universal truth. From the beginning of time, theologians have observed that by following this principle the individual is rewarded with a life of love, peace and happiness.

Love is not, as many people perceive it, some wimpy emotion. And, *romantic* love does not have a corner on the market when it comes to love. Rather than being emotionally tied to a specific person, love is a powerful force within you. The power of love is literally the force which creates and maintains the entire universe.

Universal Love is a conscious state that can be generated within you by your authentic self. It is a "state of being" you create by choice, and can enhance by simply *recognizing* the love that is already present in your life. It could be the love you feel for the members of your family, your pets, your friends, your home, or any beautiful thing in your life. This love could express as the love you have for your favorite sport or game, or the love you may have of nature. Encourage this state of love to expand within your thought atmosphere by giving your attention to it and permitting this feeling to vibrate in your being. Open up your heart to the power of Universal Love and allow this force to spill over into other areas of your life. This love carries a healing, renewing energy which may be utilized for yourself and others. See your life and those around you through the eyes of this love — and your world will begin to look a lot like heaven.

Try this little experiment: Wherever you are, wherever you go, consciously radiate love; in line at the supermarket, sitting in traffic, in your office, sitting in a theater. When you meet anyone, focus on their authentic self and your connection in Love to him or her. Treat others with kindness, love and forgiveness, and observe what happens. Kindness, love and forgiveness will return to you *multiplied!*

EXERCISE: *Forgiving Others*

☺ Give yourself 30 minutes.

1. Use the space below to write a list of everyone you need to forgive — even those with whom you may feel only a twinge of resentment.

- _____

- _____

- _____

- _____

- _____

- _____

- _____

- _____

- _____

2. Next, take a separate piece of paper and write a letter to each person, one at a time. This letter will not be sent to them — this is only for you. Write down everything this individual did to hurt you and how it made you feel. Allow the full spectrum of feelings to come up for you, including anger and sadness. Release your tears or scream into a pillow if need be. Get the feelings out and let them go.

3. After you've expressed your emotions, fold the piece of paper and hold it in your hands while saying the following prayer. Replace the words *"this person"* with the individual's name.

> *"Dear Higher Self, help me to realize that (this person) is a spiritual being having a human experience. Help me to realize that it is natural for him/her to make mistakes while he/she is learning here on Earth. (This person) did the best he/she could with the understanding they had at the time. I do not take it personally. I now forgive (this person) for every mistake I've written here. Indeed, I am only forgiving ignorance. I will remember (this person's) authentic self, even if he/she has forgotten. I now claim a new learning, a new understanding, and a blessing from that experience."*

4. Finally, burn the letter while repeating the following seven times through.

> *"I forgive. I release. I let go. I forgive. I release. I let go."*

Proceed through your list one person at a time, working through the process completely. You may want to do them all in one day, or space it out over a period of time. This exercise may not feel comfortable for you. Move forward with it anyway. The process is not about comfort, it's about healing.

EXERCISE: *Forgiving Yourself*

⊕ Give yourself 30 minutes.

Forgiving ourselves is equally important — and sometimes more difficult to do. Some of us are harder on ourselves than we could ever be on others. The toxins which our own unforgiveness creates are just as poisonous as our resentment towards others. It's time we let ourselves off the hook.

1. Write a letter to yourself, describing some of your more glaring mistakes. Do some soul-searching here. Examine if you have hurt someone either by your actions, or lack of action. Where have you been unkind? Where could you have done better? Where have you wasted your time here on Earth? Accept all the feelings that come up for you, including anger and sadness. Dig deep, then let the words flow onto the paper.

2. When you're finished, fold the piece of paper and hold it in your hands while saying the following prayer:

   "Dear Higher Self, help me to realize that I am a spiritual being having a human experience. Help me to realize it is natural for me to make mistakes while I am learning here on Earth. I did the best I could with the understanding I had at the time. Therefore, I can now forgive myself for every mistake I've written here. I forgive myself and I love myself. I now claim a new learning, a new understanding, and a blessing from each situation. Help me to see love, to experience love and to be Love."

3. Finally, burn the letter while you repeat the following seven times through:

   "I forgive. I release. I let go.
   I give the gift of forgiveness to myself."

EXERCISE : *Developing a Forgiving Attitude*

The following exercise will assist in keeping your mind clear and your heart open throughout the day. After a time, this attitude will become a central part of your thought atmosphere, attracting love and kindness from others as well as harmonious situations.

• Shortly after rising, while getting ready for the day or perhaps driving to work, repeat to your Self either silently or out loud:

> *"Dear Higher Self, please remind me, all throughout the day today, of who I truly am and why I'm really here. Help me to forgive others their mistakes and their limited vision of themselves and to behold the authentic self which lies behind this mask."*

If you genuinely desire to see the authentic loving self of everyone you meet, then that is what you will see. As you now know, we are all interconnected. Others will feel your intent on a very deep level and will respond in kind.

> "Treat people as if they were what they should be, and you help them become what they are capable of becoming."
> —*Goethe*

C HAPTER NINE

THE POWER OF MEDITATION

"Stop talking, stop thinking, and there is nothing you will not understand. Return to the Root and you will find the Meaning."
—Sengstan, Buddhist Texts

Meditation is one of the greatest tools we have available to us to immediately connect with our Higher Self — the source of all divine insight, pure love, inner wisdom and transcendent peace. Meditation is as old as time and as natural a process as breathing.

On a purely physiological level, meditation has been scientifically proven to reduce stress, calm the central nervous system, and relieve a host of problems from anxiety to sleep disorders and even drug addiction. Meditation is considered to be beneficial to the immune system which is our defense against a myriad of diseases. Meditation aids one's ability to concentrate and improves overall mental alertness. Research has found that individuals who have practiced meditation throughout their lives look eight to ten years younger than their peers. This may be because meditation gives your body and mind a *deep rest* — much more than sleep itself. For the ten, twenty or sixty minutes you spend in meditation, your entire being dwells in a state of suspended timelessness.

This sense of timelessness is another important benefit of meditation, for it gives you the opportunity to *be* entirely in the present moment. Most of us fluctuate between living in the past and in the future. We are often influenced by what just happened: "What did she mean when she said that?" "He was such a jerk to me." Or, we critique our own performance, "How did I come across?" or "I should have said...". Alternately, our present moment awareness is robbed by the enormous amounts of time we spend planning the future: "What will I wear?" "What will I do?" "What will I say?" "What will I have for dinner?" "Will he/she call?" "What will I do this weekend?" and of course, "How will this situation turn out?" Rarely do we spend much time simply being in the here and now, enjoying the fact that we are alive. After all, all we really have is this present moment. The past is gone. We cannot change it no matter how much we would like. We can plan for the future all we want, but seldom does it turn out exactly as expected. As the John Lennon song goes, *"Life is what happens while we're busy making other plans."* To be fully present in the moment, to breathe in life, to feel our oneness with the Source of all love is the experience of ecstasy. This is what meditation gives you. A wise sage once said:

"You are where your attention takes you. In fact, you *are* your attention. If your attention is fragmented, you are fragmented. When your attention is in the past, you are in the past. When your attention

133

is in the present moment, you are in the presence of God and God is present in you."

On an even deeper level, meditation will assist you in transcending the chaotic world around you for a brief period of time in order to experience Pure Being. Meditation will move you beyond all external voices and demands, as well as beyond the boundaries of the physical senses. It will transport you into the Eternal Stillness — the Source of all creation. It will help you transcend the influence of the ego, find your authentic self and once there, you will be able to hear Its voice.

Your authentic self speaks an entirely different language than that of the false self. It tells you that you are loved, that you are magnificent and perfect *right now*. Your authentic self invites you to rise above external appearances and delve into the still, peaceful timelessness of eternal Reality. This is the place where Universal Love-Intelligence has individualized Itself as you, and meditation is the means by which you may connect with It. When you do, you will be enfolded in Its limitless love and infinite peace. During meditation you understand, not in theory, but in an *experiential way,* the nature of God and the nature of your Self — which are one and the same.

Meditation is akin to fine-tuning a radio to a station that is broadcasting a beautiful symphony. Most of the time we walk around tuned into nothing but static. The act of meditation precisely tunes our "dial" to the divine station so that we may hear the angelic symphony which sings songs of our unity with Itself.

In addition, the experience of communing with this Source does not end when the meditation is over. Little by little, you take more and more of this awareness back into your waking life. As a result, you become anchored in the awareness that you *are* your authentic self regardless of the hypnotism of the collective unconscious. Life, then, can be approached from a centered position, placing everything in your world in its proper perspective.

It's easy to become distracted from the source of our being by our day-to-day life. We are constantly bombarded with messages of limitation and belief systems based on separation. Before we realize it, we've forgotten who we are and have begun capitulating to a world ruled by the false self. Meditation is our most effective remedy. In meditation we re-align with our authentic self and become as a window, or portal through which the pureness of Reality can pour through our consciousness, and into our lives.

Meditation is also extremely practical because it gives us the opportunity to go back to the Source, or First Cause behind all experience. This is where we have the opportunity to glean the pure Truth behind any situation we're currently experiencing. Anchoring with the Source of all insight and inner wisdom during daily meditation gives us the ultimate advantage in life. Not only do we see things from this higher perspective, but also, if it is our intention, we will be supplied with insight regarding a particular situation and the most effective direction we can take.

Where To Begin

The practice of meditation poses a tremendous threat to the ego because, when you become quiet, you have the opportunity to observe what this false self is up to. Meditation effectively quiets its voice, therefore your false self will fiercely resist your attempts to practice. A clue that your false self is in control might be if you notice you are waiting to find the best teacher, or the correct method, or the right time to start a meditation program. The false self will also resist your staying with a meditation program. If you notice that you are making excuses why you don't have time to meditate, or rationalizing that meditation is not really working and therefore a waste of time, be aware that this is a signal. The voice of the ego is literally fighting for its life. Who's going to win? It's up to you. Remember, your choice is between living a life dictated by the false self, or a life that is peaceful, fulfilling and miraculous.

> "It's characteristic of the ego that it takes all that is unimportant as important and all that is important as unimportant."
> —*Meher Baba*

The best way to adhere to a meditation program is to schedule a specific time each day to practice — and if you feel resistance from the false self, acknowledge it, then *consciously* make the decision to meditate anyway.

People often say to me, "But, Victoria, you see I've tried to meditate, but it doesn't work for me because I can not quiet my mind." That's like saying "I can't walk to the store, because the store is at the end of the block and I'm over here." How you walk to the store is by putting one foot in front of the other. Before you know it, you're at the store — *and* you may have had a nice time along the way! Meditation is like the process of walking: you put one foot in front of the other. Before you know it you'll get there — *and* you may have had a nice time along the way.

There's no need to focus on the *goal* of quieting the mind, focus on the *process*. If you feel at any time during meditation that your mind is wandering, don't be concerned. Everyone's mind wanders. Our heads are fully occupied with mindless thoughts all day long. In meditation, you become quiet enough to notice them. When you become aware that this is happening, that's great! Now, *gently* bring your focus back to the breath, or to thoughts of your inner self, or wherever you left off. *The act of bringing the mind back is part of the meditation itself.* In fact, some meditations are centered around the practice of mindfully observing your thoughts coming in and going out like the tide.

The best time to meditate is in the early morning before your day begins. If you can get up before your children or your spouse needs you, you'll be giving yourself a refreshing head start. Give the gift of twenty minutes to yourself. If that means getting up twenty minutes earlier, just know that twenty minutes of meditation will give you a deeper rest than an extra twenty minutes of sleep. However, make sure you are fully awake before sitting down to meditate. First, do some stretches, or take a shower or have a cup of tea. Another good time to meditate is early evening. If you practice meditation after a stressful day at work or home, those twenty minutes will turn your day around and renew you for the activities of that evening. It's certainly more beneficial than reaching for that cocktail. In fact, you most likely won't want it after you've meditated. Of course, what's even better is meditating twice a day — once in the morning and once in the evening. This program will, in effect, sandwich your day with pure love and divine insight.

Meditation Techniques:

There are a numerous types of meditation styles. A popular technique is with the use of a *mantra*, which is a universal sound that has no specific meaning and is consistently repeated throughout the meditation. The purpose of a mantra is to assist you in gently shifting your focus away from the concerns of this world to the presence within. The most commonly used mantra is *Om* (or Aum.) This is a Universal Mantra, which means that anyone can use it. The sound of Om dates back three thousand years to the ancient Vedic hymns. It is said that the word Om contains the whole world; past, present and future. And, he who meditates on Om enters into *Atman,* the God-Self within.

> "A mantra provides a boat with which you can float through your thoughts, unattached, entering subtler and subtler realms. It is a boat that steers itself — to the threshold of God."
> —Ram Dass, *Journey of Awakening*

There are also meditation training courses available that can give you your own personal mantra. Transcendental Meditation (TM), probably the best known, is well respected and suitable to Western culture (the ability to twist your body into a full lotus position is not required). TM combines effective technique with good support programs.

There are meditations techniques you can practice with eyes open, focused on a candle. There are walking meditations in which the meditator repeats a mantra while walking. Visualization meditation takes you to a beautiful, peaceful setting in your mind's eye. Devotional meditation utilizes chanting. The variety of meditation techniques is endless, and a good source for many of them is the classic Ram Dass book, *Journey of Awakening* (see Recommended Reading).

There is no need, however, to wait for the right class, the correct method, or the best teacher because meditation is actually all self-taught. The Unifying Meditation on the next few pages is a great place to begin, and you can do it right now!

> "Truth is within ourselves;
> It takes no rise from outward things,
> Whatever you may believe.
> There is an inmost center in us all, where truth abides in fulness...
> And to know rather consists in opening out a way whence the
> Imprisoned splendor may escape,than in effecting entry for
> A light supposed to be without."   —Robert Browning

EXERCISE: *Unifying Meditation*

🕐 Give yourself 20 minutes

Read the directions a few times first, then follow the steps from memory. Better still, have someone read the steps to you *slowly* while you do them. If you find it easier to follow a guided meditation on tape, the *Manifesting Your Desires: Exercises and Processes* audiocassette has this exact meditation on Side Two. (See back page to order.)

Before you begin, imagine being surrounded by a large globe of white light. Say the following affirmation to yourself: "My aura is closed to all but the highest vibration," and know that your word makes it so. This will put a protective garment of light around you, allowing you to be open only to positive energy.

If the endless stream of thoughts running through your mind begins to bother you, you may want to incorporate the following process at any time during the meditation. Practice it for a minute or two, then, slowly bring your attention back to the Unifying Meditation.

Visualize yourself resting by a peaceful stream. As you see the stream flowing along, you notice leaves floating slowly past you. Each leaf represents one of your thoughts. Simply notice the thoughts drifting by like the leaves — one at a time. See them come into view and then notice them drift away, without becoming attached to any particular one.

The Steps

Step 1. Sit either on a chair, on the sofa or cross-legged on the floor. If you're sitting on a sofa or a chair, make sure you're supported by a pillow at the small of your back to keep your spine erect. The object is to keep the spine as straight as possible so that the energy flows freely up and down its corridor. Rest your arms, palms face up, on your thighs. Close your eyes. This position might seem silly at first, but it works.

Step 2. Breathe deeply, slowly and deliberately from your diaphragm several times. Focus on the breath. Observe it entering your nostrils, traveling down your trachea, and filling up your lungs and belly. Then observe the breath moving out of your belly and lungs, moving through your trachea and out of your nostrils or mouth.

Step 3. Now, direct this breath through your body like a smooth wave of relaxation. Slowly, direct the breath into your feet, relaxing every toe, the arch and heel. Move upward as you allow this wave to relax your ankles and slowly on up through your calves. Let go of all tension there. Then direct this relaxing wave up to your knees, and then up to your thighs. Release the tension in the muscles. Let them hang limp. Now visualize this relaxed energy moving to your hips and buttocks. This wave of relaxation now moves slowly up into the small of your back and around to your lower abdomen. Let your stomach muscles go. Observe this wave as it travels further up, relaxing your chest, and upper back. Breathe relaxation into your entire torso. Now let this wave of relaxation flow into your shoulders, between your shoulder blades, to the top of the shoulders and down into the upper arms, elbows and forearms. Direct this relaxation into your wrists hands, and then through every finger. Allow the wave to slowly melt the muscles of your neck — the back, the sides and the front of your neck. Follow it on up to your jaw — let your jaw go limp; then your chin, mouth, cheeks, eyes, eyelids and eyebrows. Finally, feel this relaxation flow into your forehead as it smoothes out the tension lines and moves up into your scalp and around to the back of your neck.

Step 4. You should feel pretty relaxed by now. Move your attention to the breath again. Allow the breath to form the sound of Om — pronounced as A-U-M. Breathe in, then slowly breathe out, "Aaaauuuuuummmmmm." Again, breathe in, and slowly breathe out "Aaaauuuuuummmmmm." You can do this silently or out loud. Repeat this over and over, focusing on the variations of the sound of A-U-M.

Step 5. Now, when you breathe in, visualize a ball of beautiful light six inches or so above your head. When you breathe out, visualize a beam of this light channeling down through the crown of your head, and out of your mouth with every breath. Breathe in this light of your Higher Self and let it vibrate in your head. Feel the ball of white light moving closer with each breath you take until it touches your head. Then breathe it into your body. The light has now become you. You are the illumination of the Light.

Step 6. Now, repeat the following to yourself slowly, concentrating on each statement, allowing the words to vibrate in your soul for a moment before moving on to the next.

> *"Spirit has found a place to express Itself, and that is as me."*
>> *"That which I am is God in me, as me."*
>> *"God is as me, Love."*
>> *"God is as me, Peace."*
>> *"God is as me, Joy."*
>> *"God is as me Beauty & Magnificence*
>> *"God is as me, Abundance of good."*

140

"God is as me, Wholeness."

"I am that which Thou art. Thou art that which I am.
All that the Father is, I am. All that the Father has is mine.
I am the Impersonal—personalized."

Step 7. Now allow yourself to do nothing but listen. What is your Inner Self telling you? Sit and feel the peace. Listen to its voice for a while.

Step 8. When this process feels complete to you, open your eyes. Stretch your body and bring your awareness back to the room and to this world.

That's it, you've done it! You may have experienced a deep feeling of peace during this meditation, and you may not have felt anything at all. Regardless of whether or not you feel anything during meditation, *something profound is still happening.* Trust the process. As you continue to practice, it will become easier, feel more natural, and you will begin to hear the voice of your authentic self more clearly.

C HAPTER TEN

TREATMENT

"And all things, whatsoever ye shall ask in prayer,
believing, ye shall receive."

(Mt. 12:22)

In the preceding chapters you have learned that there is a definite principle in the Universe, or Law, which responds to our beliefs by reflecting them back into our lives as form and experience. Throughout this book you have been building a foundation of understanding while applying spiritual principle to your every day life. You have learned how to set your intention, shift your core beliefs, change your thought atmosphere, and weed your mental garden of resentment. In addition, you've been building your spiritual muscles through daily affirmation and meditation. By completing the exercises and processes in this workbook you have taken metaphysical theory and put it into personal practice. Perhaps you've already begun to experience profound transformation as a result. If so, congratulations! This firm foundation of understanding, which you have been building through your experience with this workbook, is precisely what is required to *activate* the process you will now be learning in this chapter.

There is a scientific method and definite technique for the manifestation of any specific desire: it is known as "spiritual mind treatment," or simply "treatment." The concept of treatment dates back to the birth of the New Thought movement in the mid-1800s. Its founders included independent thinkers such as Phineas Quimby, Warren Felt Evans and Mary Baker Eddy in America and Judge Thomas Troward in Great Britain, among others. These pioneers of New Thought took the ideas expressed by the Transcendentalists, combined them with the basic concept of prayer, and developed a formula with provable results. The spiritual mind treatment technique has been refined over the years with each faction of the New Thought movement having its own particular version. The version shared here is closest to that taught in Religious Science founded by Ernest Holmes in the 1920s.

The term "treatment" refers to the original use of the technique by practitioners of the science, which was as an alternative treatment for healing disease. Nearly every leader in the New Thought movement became convinced of the power of treatment because they had experienced a dramatic physical healing in their lives utilizing the technique.

In essence, treatment is a step-by-step process for unifying ourselves with the creative Power of the Universe, embracing our spiritual reality and — once in alignment with this power center — claiming and accepting our specific good. Our word spoken from this pure core of our being then channels unformed substance into specific form.

As previously discussed, all form and experience are created from an idea — whether it's God's idea, or *our* idea as co-creator with the Infinite. The form or experience is the *effect* while the idea, or belief, behind it is the *cause*. For example, the experience of illness is created by a belief that disease is powerful and our body is victim to it. The belief in disease is the *cause* and the experience of illness is the *effect*. In treatment we treat the *cause*, not the effect. Our work is done internally by unifying with the One Creative Power which can know only wholeness and perfection. We then delete from our "mental computers" the belief in disease, and insert the knowledge that our body is Divine Intelligence in form. We then release the treatment to the Law which takes care of the details on the material plane.

We do not focus on changing the *form* the illness has taken in our lives, because to do so would be to fix it more firmly in our minds. This might tempt us to think of the condition as a permanent reality with which we have to struggle. When we fully realize that there are no *effects* in our "outer world" independent of a *cause* in our "inner world" we have begun to embrace the consciousness that heals.

For treatment work to be effective, we must see all experiences and conditions for what they actually are — temporary manifestations of thought forms. Our job is to mentally transmute the form or experience back to the cause — the belief which created it — then embrace a greater idea, God's idea of wholeness.

We Are Co-creators

We were each given the gift of dominion. From the beginning, mankind has misunderstood the concept of dominion to mean supremacy over the earth — as if we were given permission to rape and pillage our planet. This was never the intention of this instruction. The instruction is that we were given dominion over *our lives*. We were empowered by our Creator to co-create.

Because we are the only species which has the capacity to self-contemplate and to imagine various possible futures, we have the ability to co-create the life we desire. We have dominion over unformed substance, which is all around us, waiting for our instruction to become what *we* decide. Emma Curtis Hopkins tells us:

"It is our business to translate the Spiritual Truth within into visible manifestation."

Thomas Troward wrote the following about treatment:

"We must always bear in mind that we are dealing with a wonderful potential energy which is not yet differentiated into any particular mode and that by the action of our mind we can differentiate it into any specific mode of activity that we will; and by keeping our thought fixed on the fact that the inflow of this energy is taking place and that by our mental attitude we are determining its direction, we shall gradually realize a corresponding externalization."

Later, Ernest Holmes, who had been a student of both of these New Thought leaders, described the treatment process in his masterwork, *The Science of Mind:*

"The entire order is one of spontaneous being and spontaneous manifestation. The Law follows the word just as the word follows the desire. The desire arises from the necessity of the Universe to become self-expressed. The word gives form to Substance and the Principle of Subjective Law produces the manifestation. There is no effort in the process."

Our ability to create the life of our dreams is a natural process for us. When we understand how treatment works, it becomes a powerful tool which we may utilize to manifest our heart's desires.

Treatment is a precise scientific prayer designed to call forth from the Absolute that which you desire in manifest form.

Occasionally, the words *treatment* and *prayer* are used interchangeably and, within the pages of this book, they mean similar things. However, the word *prayer*, as commonly understood, has an entirely different meaning. For most, prayer is an act supplication, where one beseeches an external power to intervene on their behalf. Many pray to a God outside themselves to help change a situation which has become unbearable. Often people pray only out of desperation, when everything else they've tried has failed. This type of praying reinforces the false notion that the Power of God is outside of them. It keeps them trapped in a consciousness of victimhood.

With that said, it is true that there are times when falling to our knees and asking a Higher Power to fill us with peace and understanding is entirely appropriate. However, this Higher Power, which is universal, is also very much *inside* of us, *"closer than breathing, nearer than hands or feet."* Treatment is so effective because it unifies us with the Source of all good — that Power which individualizes as us. When we embrace our connection with the Divine, we're able to pray with an understanding of our innate power. This understanding is the power that produces results.

> "Prayer is the contemplation of the facts of life from the Highest Point of View."
>
> —*Ralph Waldo Emerson*

In a sense, treatment uncovers the absolute Truth about us. Out of our misunderstanding of who and what we are, we have created many forms and experiences which obscure the fundamental Reality behind the appearance. Treatment then is a process for uncovering the "spiritual prototype" of perfection inherent in any situation or condition. Ernest Holmes explains this in *How To Use The Science of Mind:*

> "[One's] entire treatment is based on the assumption that there is a spiritual pattern at the center of everything. The perfect was always there, it was implanted by the Spirit. The imperfect has been added by the human mind. What the human mind has put there, it can take away. What the Divine has implanted cannot be uprooted; it can only appear to be covered up. Spiritual mind practice is an uncovering of the Divine Nature."

We can think of treatment as a process of uncovering the good that has always been there and *is there now*, awaiting our recognition. In a very real sense we are clearing away the debris which is covering up the perfection and beauty that lie hidden within.

Analogy:

> Imagine that you are mining for diamonds in a new mine reported to be laden with beautiful stones. You've never done this before, but you go with an experienced friend. Your friend believes there is a real possibility that diamonds can be found in the mine. However, once inside the shaft, all *you* see is dirt. Your friend picks up a seemingly worthless clod of dirt and exclaims, "Look at all these diamonds!" You don't believe him because all you see is the dirt clod. When you come back up to the surface, your friend takes that dirt clod and digs away at it. He scrapes and washes it. Suddenly you see a shimmer. After more scrubbing and chiseling, you finally see a sparkling diamond. It was there all the time, surrounded by worthless dirt, its beauty hidden from view.

The Five Steps of Treatment

Following are the five steps of treatment:

- **Recognition**

- **Unification**

- **Realization**

- **Thanksgiving**

- **Release**

It might be helpful (and fun) to remember the steps of treatment by its acronym, RURTR, as in Rotor Rooter. The Rotor Rooter process unblocks drains to allow water to flow freely. Similarly, the RURTR treatment unblocks consciousness to allow the Absolute Truth to flow freely into our lives.

Before you begin, state your purpose for the treatment. For example, if you are experiencing financial lack, you might say, "The purpose of this treatment is to realize financial abundance in my life." If you are looking to find the man or woman of your dreams you might say, "The purpose of this treatment is to realize love and to experience a committed, loving relationship with a man (or woman)." If you are unhappy or depressed you might state your purpose as, "To realize and experience more joy in every area of my life." If you're experiencing career failure or unfulfillment you might say, "The purpose of this treatment is to realize a fulfilling and successful career doing what I love." Be specific, but don't outline. Be open to accept something even greater than you can imagine.

Instructions For Each Step

Step 1: Recognition

The first step is to recognize that God is all there is. Either visualize or say aloud words that will help you remember the all-inclusive nature of God. Know that there is only one Power, one Presence, one Energy, one Intelligence, and one Life. This is the Love-Intelligence which creates, guides and governs the universe. This one Life exists both in an unformed state as well as expressing Itself as form. Recognize that there is only one Spirit which individualizes as each and every person. State the qualities of this Spirit: pure love, pure joy and happiness, infinite peace, exquisite beauty and magnificence, absolute perfection, unboundedness and unlimited abundance of all good. Recognize that because Spirit is the only presence, all the qualities of Spirit are omnipresent — and this includes the situation or condition for which you are treating. Ernest Holmes writes in *The Science of Mind*, "Since Spirit is present in its entirety at all times and in all places, it follows that all of Spirit is wherever we center our attention." There is no opposing power and no place where God — and all of Its qualities — is not.

Step 2: Unification

In this step you consciously connect with the Power. You will personalize the knowledge that God is all there is. Because there is only one Spirit, acknowledge that you are an integral part of this Spirit. State that you are the Impersonal—*personalized*. Know that the Universe has chosen to individualize Itself as you in order to express its magnificence. God breathes forth life *as you* in order to experience life in this three-dimensional plane. State that the allness, wholeness and completeness of the Infinite expresses as you. Therefore, you are the self-extension of limitless love, pure joy and unbounded happiness. You are a unique expression of infinite peace, beauty and magnificence, absolute perfection, unlimited intelligence, creativity and abundance. There is, in fact, no place where Spirit leaves off and you begin. All that God is, you are. All that God has is yours now. Recognize that this is your true self and the reality of you *now* — no matter what the appearance may be at the moment. Feel your oneness with Infinite Spirit. Let it fill your entire being. Let this fullness resonate in your soul.

Also in this step, you want to remember that you are a co-creator with the Universe. Understand that the Power to co-create a magnificent life is yours by Divine right! Know that the power *God* uses to create the Universe is the same Power *you* are using now. God is Macrocosm and you are microcosm. Your treatment is the *activity* of God's will in you. Accept this Truth all the way down to the core of your being. Recognize that you are an individualized thinking center within Universal Creative Intelligence. Because you are the Impersonal—*personalized,* the words you are speaking in this treatment are the words of pure Spirit in you.

Step 3: Realization

The stage has been set — and now is the time to speak your word and claim your specific good. This is where you get to use your imagination and creativity, so be specific and detailed. Also, be sure to engage your *feeling nature.* For example: How would you feel if you had what you desired in your life right now? Add color, texture and warmth. Make the picture real for yourself. Run the movie in your head. What would you be doing? What would you be experiencing? Enjoy and embrace these images. Allow the joy to well up within your soul.

In this step you acknowledge the good the Universe has already given you, and *allow* it to manifest in your life. Claim and accept your good as if it were yours now — for it is! Because what you are claiming is your heart's desire for good in your life, it is God's will for you. And, if it is God's will, then it is already an accomplished fact. Behind the thin veil of appearance (which are your old beliefs in form) *there has always been, and is now, a perfect, beloved, harmonious, joyous, prosperous and successful person.* This is your authentic self. Your desired good is a spiritual Reality, first created in and by Spirit, and now accepted within your consciousness. Because all things are first *thoughts,* what you are claiming is a thought now in process of becoming a thing.

To sense that you already *have* your good *now* is an essential element in the treatment sequence. Remember, a feeling of need will only manifest more need. What you are doing in this step is moving from a sense of need to an *awareness of having*. Enjoy the feeling of *having* that which you have just claimed. Confidently accept that you now have the fulfillment of your desire!

Step 4: Thanksgiving

After you have accepted your good, you must now give thanks with every fiber of your being. Rejoice that what you have just claimed is now a Reality in your life. Give thanks for the awakening in your consciousness of who and what you really are — the self-expression of the allness, wholeness and completeness of God. Be grateful for the *knowledge* of the power of your word in your life. Truly, this knowledge has set you free! Give thanks for the *awareness* that this specific good is already yours now. Generate this feeling of gratitude by imagining your entire being vibrating with love.

Step 5: Release

In this final step, you will release the treatment to the Law, knowing you have done your part of the treatment sequence and are now allowing Creative Intelligence to simply take care of the details. Its role is to take what you have just claimed — which is currently in a spiritual and mental form — and clothe it in material form and experience. Know that this Law is the Infinite organizing power which brings about the perfect situations, healing, contacts and opportunities into manifestation. Remember that the Law is subject to the Spirit, and you are Spirit. For certainly when Spirit says "Let there be Light," there is light; and when Spirit in you, *as you,* says "Let there be fulfillment," there is fulfillment.

At the end of the treatment there should be a sense of completion, a feeling that it's a "done deal!" Understand that the word you have just spoken (out of your conscious connection with Love-Intelligence) has created a new reality. Your word, spoken with this awareness *is the thing itself.* It's not going to *become* the thing, it *is* the thing. Therefore, declare with confidence: "And so it is!"

Case Study: Wanda

Wanda has been bouncing around from job to job searching in vain to find a position that is well paying, satisfying, stimulating, relaxed and creative. She has been fired from two jobs for her lack of focus and initiative. Wanda feels she was treated unfairly both times, but she does admit she intensely disliked the two jobs.

The first thing Wanda must address is the issue of forgiveness. Her task is to release the situations and the people she feels are responsible for her firing (refer to Chapter Nine.) Then she must claim a blessing from each job she has ever held. This will effectively weed her mental garden and clear the ground for new good to grow. If she skips this step, the weeds of resentment will continue to block the flow of her good. The next step she must take is to clarify her vision by completing the "Exercise for Defining and Clarifying Your True Desires."

With the forgiveness exercise complete, Wanda now has an understanding that each job, including the two from which she was fired, has taught her a valuable skill she will be able to use in her "dream job." In addition, Wanda has more clarity about what her ideal job will look like. She is now ready to begin the treatment process.

Example: Wanda's Treatment

"The purpose of this treatment is to realize and experience a joyous, fulfilling and successful career."

Recognition:

"I recognize that God is all there is: the one Power, one Presence, one Spirit and one Life. This Life is pure joy, pure love and infinite abundance. All of the qualities of the Universe are everywhere present in their fullness. This one Love-Intelligence creates, guides and governs everything in the Universe. This one Spirit is the great Impersonal which personalizes as each one of us in order to express Itself."

Unification:

"I am this Impersonal personalized. The allness, wholeness and completeness of Universal God individualizes as me in order to express Its magnificence. I am the self-expression of God's love, joy, creativity and intelligence. The Universe fulfills itself *through* me and *as* me. This one Life which is *my* life is joyous, successful and glorious! I also know that I am a co-creator with the Infinite. Because I am this I AM, the word that I speak is the word of Spirit through me and as me." (She breathes this Truth in and allows it to vibrate within her soul.)

Realization:

"It is my Divine heritage to be fulfilled and successful expressing my unique talents, therefore I accept and embrace this birthright now. I now claim and accept the Truth that the perfect, joyous and fulfilling career is mine now. This successful career where my unique talents and gifts are being expressed is unfolding perfectly now. I am surrounded by supportive and harmonious people. I am confident in, recognized for, and rewarded for my talents. I am being well compensated for my contribution. All are blessed by who I am and what I do." (Wanda spends a few moments feeling what this situation would be like for her. She sees what her work environment looks like. She sees her co-workers smiling and helpful. She feels fulfilled expressing her talents. She feels excited about going to work in the morning, etc. She drinks in the joy of having her perfect career expression now. After generating this feeling-tone, Wanda now continues speaking her word.) "I am God's living enterprise, therefore I am already a success! I accept that this fulfilling and successful career is mine now, and I am open and receptive to the divine guidance and intuition which is guiding me every step of the way."

Thanksgiving:

"I now give abundant thanks for the re-awakening in my consciousness of who and what I really am. I give thanks that this is already the truth about me. I am grateful that I don't need to make it happen, it is already *mine now*, and it is unfolding flawlessly. For this awareness I am filled with gratitude." Wanda takes a moment to breathe in the feeling of love and gratitude.

Release:

"I release this word into the Law, with absolute confidence that Universal Intelligence simply takes care of the details. It is done. And so it is!"

At this point Wanda lets go of the treatment with calm assurance that infinite organizing power is now actively at work bringing about the situations and circumstances based on this realization. Her task now is to listen to the inner voice within her and to take action following its guidance. (The next chapter, *Inspired Action* will reveal the instructions for how this is done.)

General Guidelines for Effective Treatments

♦ You do not need to use the precise words or phrases above. In fact, stating these ideas in your own language will make the treatment more personal. Also, treatment said out loud tends to be more effective. The spoken word is clearer and more focused, hence more powerful.

♦ You will have the best results with treatment if you follow the steps in the order indicated. Successful treatment needs a proper foundation. For the first two steps of treatment, it is important to capture a feeling of oneness with your Source. The goal here is to capture a deep understanding that Love-Intelligence *is your identity*. Then, when you move on to the Realization step, you are speaking your word from your Divine Center.

The following wisdom is from author, teacher and founder of The Quartus Foundation, John Randolph Price, reprinted by permission from his book, *Practical Spirituality*. He addresses the importance of first identifying with Spirit:

> "Words spoken from a spiritual consciousness have power to mold substance and create positive experiences. "Spiritual consciousness" means being in tune with Spirit — the state of mind and heart that you feel when you have gone within and have touched the Light. When you are in this higher consciousness and speak the word with a clearly-defined purpose, you are establishing a particular vibration in substance. And as this vibration is "stepped down" it becomes a force field that manifests in visible forms and conditions according to the Idea behind the spoken word."

♦ Remember, this is not a process of using will power to "make something happen." There should be no strain or force involved in the process. As Troward explains in his book, *The Edinburgh Lectures:*

> "If, using the word in its widest sense, we may say that the imagination is the creative function, we may call the will the centralizing principle. Its function is to keep the imagination centered in the right direction."

♦ Understand that you do not create the energy — it's already there. What you are doing is directing it with your thoughts. The irony is you've been doing this all along — only unconsciously — and often directing this energy in undesirable ways.

♦ In general, do not define where your good should come from. Let the Intelligence of the Universe take care of that. It has a bigger picture. In fact,

156

when you are claiming a specific thing in treatment (i.e., for a certain job), it's important to say *"this, or better, God."* This gives Universal Intelligence permission to give you something even more magnificent than you can imagine for yourself. If the specific good you claimed does not show up the way you intended, *trust that the Universe is in the process of bringing you something even better!*

♦ The importance of giving thanks for your good, even before it manifests in visible form, cannot be stressed enough. If you *wait* until your good manifests to give thanks, it won't. The key to successful treatments is to express gratitude when the good is in the invisible state (Step 4). It's not that God is waiting for you to be polite, it's that an attitude of gratitude creates within you a feeling of having, which acts as a magnet for your good.

> "The important point to remember is to be grateful not for any form of good but for the Spirit which underlies that form, the Spirit which produces that form."
> *—Joel Goldsmith*

What can you "treat" for?

You can treat for absolutely anything that would bring good into your life without hurting yourself or coercing another individual.

A few examples might be:

- A more fulfilling, higher paying job
- A harmonious and joyous day
- A loving relationship
- An active social life
- Relief from depression
- Peace of mind
- Divine guidance / wisdom

- Material good of any kind. Anything that would add beauty, ease and joy to your life.
- More financial abundance. As much as you can accept for yourself.
- Healing of illness
- Doing well on an interview or an exam
- A new home

There are a few purposes for which spiritual mind treatment is *not* recommended. These include:

- Changing another person's behavior. For example, you cannot treat to make your kids want to behave. You *can*, however, treat for a harmonious family life. That's a divine birthright. The healing happens first within you. As a result, those around you are lifted.

- Misfortune of any kind for someone else. Remember the Law of Karma — desiring ill for anyone will cause it to return to *you*.

- Treating for a specific person to be your mate. Everyone has free will, and coercion or manipulation only leads to deeper unhappiness. You *can* treat for a companion who possesses the qualities you admire in that specific person.

Common Questions:

When is the best time to do a treatment?

Ideally, directly after meditation. The reason is that you are already in a state which is receptive to Universal Intelligence and are experiencing your oneness with It. Therefore, when you do the treatment after meditation you don't have to work hard to convince yourself of the Truth — you feel it naturally. Also, in meditation you are in direct contact with the Infinite Substance from which all form and experience issue. Once there, you simply present your "mold" (the desire you are claiming in treatment) to Unformed Substance which pours itself through to become form.

However, if it's not convenient to do your treatment after meditation, then find that five to ten minutes of uninterrupted time at another point in the day. Some people do treatments in the shower, while getting dressed, in the car, or while jogging or bicycling. If you can be fully attentive to the treatment while performing a repetitive task, this is okay. However, you will reap fruitful rewards if you make it a priority to sit down and give your complete attention to the treatment. A good time to do this might be just before going to sleep at night. The last thought spilling into your subconscious will be your acceptance of good!

How often should I do a treatment?

In truth, once you do an effective treatment, it is already in the process of manifesting. However, after a day or so, many people lose the conviction they had during the first treatment, and begin to doubt that the good they claimed is truly theirs. This ensuing doubt renders the treatment impotent. Hence, the need to treat once a day until the good is in visible form. Think of it as wearing a retainer after the braces come off. If you neglect wearing the retainer, your teeth will shift back to their original shape.

Also, do one treatment at a time for each desire. When that goal has been accomplished, move on to the next one. Start with "simple" goals to build your faith, then move on to the "larger" issues. In Truth, there is no large or small, and the Universe can manifest a million dollars as easily as a hundred dollars. However, treating and accepting your good in increments helps to build your faith that this process works. Think of it as constructing a history of success. Recognize and rejoice in each achievement.

How long will my good take to manifest?

In essence, every treatment works immediately. The treatment itself *is the essence* of the manifest form or experience. The time it takes for the actual form to appear will vary according to your level of acceptance and the natural process of physical unfoldment. If you believe it can happen immediately then it *will* happen immediately. Many demonstrations are made right after the first treatment. This is especially true if you require an immediate demonstration, such as treating for a meeting or an interview to go well, or to pass a test, or to heal a cold because of an upcoming event, etc. Don't be surprised if your phone rings with the good news even before you finish the treatment!

On the other hand, if there are long-standing conflicting core beliefs around the issue you're treating, this may slow the process down. In that case, recognize that every treatment you do is moving you one step closer to your acceptance of the good which has already been given to you. You may find it helpful to return to the chapter on Core Beliefs and redo the exercises.

Keep in mind you want to avoid anxiously awaiting for your good to arrive. Do not concentrate on the outward results. Remember, what you are looking to accomplish in treatment is the *feeling* that your good is already here. Your treatment is effective when you have completely released it to the Law, knowing it is a current reality. *"Before they call, I will answer."* Do not make the mistake of thinking your good will come next month, next week, or even tomorrow. If you do, you will be postponing your good and putting it into a state of futurity which can never come to pass. Even if you're treating for a specific thing like a car for example, know that the car already exists, is yours now, and that Infinite Organizing Power is working *this moment* to bring it into your life.

Why isn't my good manifesting?

Troward tells us, "The Law is always the same, that our thought forms a spiritual prototype which, *if left undisturbed,* will reproduce itself in external circumstances." The key words here are "if left undisturbed." If you are doing treatments and meditating faithfully every day for a period of time and your good still hasn't manifested, then check your inner dialogue throughout the day. What sometimes happens is that later in the day, after you've completed your treatment, conflicting thoughts may creep into your consciousness to undermine the manifestation process.

See if you recognize any of the following negative characters. Old Mr. Doubt says "Oh yeah, you think so, huh? Have you forgotten the odds are against you? Maybe you're just indulging in wishful thinking." Then there's mean Mr. Fear. He works deeply on your emotions to convince you that the worst could happen. Perhaps Mr. "Reality" comes to tell you that the "reality" of the situation is absolutely opposite to what you've claimed and, of course, you can't change "reality." Does Ms. Unworthy pay you a visit? Her schpiel is that you don't deserve this particular good. "Who do you think you are, anyway?!" These characters are the various voices of your "false self," the part of you that wants to keep you small. If you let these voices convince you of their erroneous perceptions, it will, in effect, cancel the original treatment.

If you're troubled by doubt after the treatment, go back and redo the exercises in the chapters, "False Self/Authentic Self" and "Core Beliefs." Remember, a good method for keeping your consciousness clear throughout the day is to do your affirmations. Affirmations will effectively realign you back to center. They remind you that, contrary to what your negative voices have to say, you are actually God in expression and you are standing in the center in your good now.

With that said, there is a phenomenon which occasionally occurs. Sometimes we *unconsciously* give ourselves an illness or discordant condition because there is something important we need to learn about ourselves through the experience. The difficult condition remains with us until we learn the lesson.

Example:

Until recently, I'd been plagued for years with a chronic digestive condition which, much to my frustration, was not responding to spiritual mind treatment. I could not understand this, because everything I had ever treated for demonstrated. After working with my practitioner, I discovered that there was an important lesson I was to learn.

I had a tendency to move very fast, always looking to get to my destination. I would ignore the importance of surrendering into the perfection of the moment, and get impatient easily. There was generally a lot of resistance going on within me and it was manifesting as an uncooperative digestive system. It took some effort retraining a life long habit, but it was necessary if I was going to live a normal life. Once I understood what the lesson was, and began working with it diligently, the digestive condition responded to spiritual mind treatment and cleared up within a couple of weeks. Every day I'm learning to let go more and more and trust that everything is working out in perfect time. Occasionally my tummy still gives me a signal to slow down, let go and enjoy the moment.

It's clear to me that I would not have learned this valuable lesson if it were not for the illness. Therefore, ultimately the condition was a blessing for me as my enjoyment of life has increased a hundred fold.

What is the role of faith in treatment?

Faith is necessary, but a new definition for the word is in order. Faith does not mean hope, nor is it blind. Faith is *visionary.* One of the many remarkable things Ernest Holmes wrote was: *"Faith looks to the invisible and instead of seeing a void, it fastens its gaze upon a solid reality."* Faith should be an acknowledgment that what we are claiming for ourselves is already ours *even though we can not yet see it.* Faith is hearing God's "Yes" when everyone else is saying "No." It is knowing in our heart that the Universe is *for* us. It is the awareness that we are using a scientific Principle to direct the Power for Good in our life. It is recognizing that our good is in the process of manifesting, no matter how it looks at the moment.

> "Now faith is the substance of things hoped for, as it was the substance of things which have come to pass; and it is the evidence of things not seen."
>
> *—Hebrews 11:1*

If I use spiritual mind treatment, can I forgo medical treatment?

A Course in Miracles states, "I am under no Law but God's." Indeed, no doctor's opinion, parent's opinion, lack of formal education, bank statement, unemployment figures, chronological-age charts, statistics, or any other form of external limitation has any genuine effect on you *unless you give it the power to do so.*

However, this does not mean that once you've completed your treatment, you can ignore your doctor's advice and stop taking medication. For God works in mysterious ways and can work miracles through your physician's hands, through a pill, through the words of a friend, or by following a healthy diet. Indeed,

God's work is often-times accomplished through others. Do not ignore the many ways in which healing can occur. The best advice is to listen to your inner wisdom, which will inspire you to make the correct choice.

Example:

> When I was a teenager, I had 20/200 eyesight and couldn't see past the end of my nose. I hated wearing glasses and could not tolerate contact lenses for long periods of time, so I treated for perfect vision. I had such faith in the power of treatment, I was convinced that when I opened my eyes, I would see perfectly. I was surprised when I didn't, but, this did not shake my faith. I knew there was a way. (The great thing about being naive is that you haven't yet heard the world tell you it's impossible.) Anyway, I continued to treat. Before long, I was given the name of an eye doctor who was experimenting with contact lenses that, like braces on teeth, reshaped the cornea of the eye. Once perfect vision was restored, the patient would need only wear the lenses a few hours a week, like a retainer. The process is called *orthokeratology* and, at the time, there was only one doctor in the U.S. who was utilizing it. As "fate" would have it, he had an office in my home town. Following divine guidance, I signed up and two years later, my vision was completely corrected.

> Even though I had assumed my eyesight would be corrected by a "miracle", I didn't realize the miracle was actually an obscure ophthalmologic procedure that I was divinely guided to investigate. Now, it's entirely possible *you* could have a spontaneous healing for whatever you're treating — many people do. If not, you will be led to take whatever the right course is for you.

EXERCISE: *Your Own Treatment*

Think of a desire you would like to see manifest. Create a purpose statement with that goal in mind. Next, using the template below, write a treatment in your own words for this desired good. Be sure to include in each section the ideas listed in the RURTR treatment above. Feel free to photocopy these two pages to use for additional treatments.

Purpose Statement:

_____

_____

Recognition:

_____

_____

_____

_____

_____

_____

Unification:

_____

_____

_____

_____

Realization:

_____

_____

_____

_____

_____

_____

Thanksgiving:

_____

_____

_____

Release:

_____

_____

_____

And so it is!

165

C HAPTER ELEVEN

INSPIRED ACTION

"Let us go now and wake up our luck."
—Ancient proverb

The proverb quoted on the proceeding chapter page is short, but rich with instruction. It tells us that our "luck" (our success, our good fortune) is already here — it only needs to be awakened. And how do we awaken it? By "going," or taking action, it instructs us. When is the best time to do this? "Now!" Wisdom indeed. Let us take action now, following our inner guidance to facilitate the manifestation of our true desires.

Many perceive Jesus' instruction to us, "Seek ye first the kingdom of Heaven and all things will be added unto you," as proof that taking no outward action in the world is the path he was indicating. This approach is occasionally favored in the spiritual community. Some on the spiritual path believe that if they meditate, pray and behave spiritually, everything they could ever need will be provided for them. While this is indeed *part* of the formula, we must also remember that we are spiritual beings living in *a human, material world*.

> "We are spirits, in the material world."
> —*Sting*

Just as some forget that we are spiritual beings, others overlook the fact that we are living in the material world. A thorough understanding that we are spiritual beings would be all that we'd need *if* we were simply spirits *not* living in this three-dimensional, material world. There are two parts to the equation, each equally important. When we embrace both, we will experience true wholeness.

For example, there are some individuals who are the most loving and giving people you'll ever meet — but alas, they can't pay their rent. Around the first of every month they go into a panic, start praying, and then perhaps begin to ask their friends or family for a loan. After they receive it, they assume their prayer was answered and they were, once again, provided for. While this may be true, it does not replace a commitment to being financially responsible.

Yes, the Truth is that the Infinite is the source of all of our supply, all our good. However, treating to realize that we are sourced by God and then sitting back expecting bags of gold to appear on our doorstep, is not spiritual growth. Manna from heaven comes through jobs and opportunities we're instructed to take. Therefore, the second part of the equation: "we are living in a material world" means *acting upon* the divine guidance we have received in the silence.

It is true that God will add all things unto us, *but the Power can work for us only as It works through us.* The importance of seeking the Kingdom first is in connecting with our true nature which is the source of all our good, including our inner guidance. It is essential that those of us on the spiritual path understand that we are here to express God's love through our beingness *and* through our doingness. We have all been given unique skills, talents and abilities which the Universe *uses* to give of Itself to the world. Using our God-given abilities creates an energy of circulation for which we are well compensated in many ways.

Once you have connected with the Source within you, divine guidance and inspiration will be revealed to you. You will be led to know what to do *in the material world.* This is sometimes called "Treat and move your feet." This guidance might be to apply for a specific job, to join a health club, to give someone a call, or to charge a specific amount for your services. It could be to mentally and spiritually prepare for an interview or team up with a partner. It might be to update your resume, take out an ad in the personals, hire a part time assistant, or join a civic organization. In any case, your inner wisdom will tell you exactly what to do. Your job is to listen in the silence and then take action — and continue to take action until you're guided to do something else. When you combine daily spiritual practices and daily Divinely guided activity, you are integrating both parts of the equation. Following this formula ensures both spiritual and tangible fulfillment.

> "High achievers spot rich opportunities swiftly, make big decisions quickly, and move into action immediately. Follow these principles and you can make your dreams come true."
> —*Dr. Robert Schuller*

Developing Your Intuition:

Following are steps to develop a strong relationship with your inner wisdom.

1. Go into the silence either through meditation or by simply closing your eyes and consciously connecting with your higher self.

2. Ask the question, "What do *I* need to do in the material world to facilitate the birth of my dream?"

170

3. Listen. You may receive the answer right away in meditation — and it may be as clear as if someone whispered in your ear.

If not, pick up a pen and take out your journal. Ask the question again. You may want to print the question on the top of the page. Then, start writing — allowing your inner self to spell the words out for you.

Also, the answer you need may come later. A similar phenomenon occurs when you forget a person's name. While you're concentrating on remembering the name, your mind is constricted. Later, after you've let it go and are focusing on something else, the name spontaneously comes to mind. Similarly, as you focus on other activities, the answer will oftentimes pop into your mind. It may be two days after you've made the request, and you could be sitting in a waiting room reading an old issue of *Time*. Perhaps you see something that triggers the subconscious — and suddenly the answer bursts out of you, "That's what I need to do, set a dinner meeting with so and so!" Others may look at you like you've lost your marbles but you just smile to yourself, knowing that this is indeed the guidance you had requested.

4. Once you've received the first instruction — even if it doesn't seem to make sense at the moment, or fit into your other plans — act upon it. You must trust enough to take the first step.

5. Generally, only after you've followed the first instruction will you be given the next step. You then take action on this new instruction. Soon, you'll be given another, and so on. Before you know it you're walking on a clearly marked path, your goal plainly in view.

This is how you build a relationship with your inner wisdom. It will not fail you. Also, your inspired action will be far more productive than your own self-initiated plans. America is busy nation peopled with individuals who run around doing many things, but do not necessarily get anywhere. When your activity is self-initiated (i.e., not divinely inspired) it is oftentimes confused and ineffective. When you allow the Divine Wisdom within you to guide your every step, you move out into the world on purpose and achieve far more.

The Power of Persistence

Many people will, after trying something for awhile, tend to give up when the road gets bumpy or a little too steep. Some might rationalize that their true desire must not be what God wanted them to do — implying that if the Universe had intended it for them, It would have made the goal easier to attain. This is not necessarily so. Perhaps the Universe wants you to develop and expand an aspect of yourself so that you may become more whole. For example, perhaps you discover after a few months of pursuing your dream that it requires financial skills, and you've never been talented at math. Maybe your true desire requires you to speak before large groups of people and you've always been petrified of public speaking. Perhaps you've discovered your dream requires management skills and you're sure you are not good at supervising people. Your heart's desire could possibly require you to take a "day job" until your dream career yields an income. If so, is that "day job" developing new skills you will need later? Maybe the relationship of your dreams is suddenly requiring much more work than you anticipated.

Does this mean that your heart's desire was incorrect? Did God make a mistake by choosing you to do this particular thing? No! You were given a desire in your heart because growth and expansion are what the Universe is about. Trust that the Universe knows what it is doing. Trust your heart.

You can bet that if you're terrified of trying something new which requires a skill you don't think you have — then you possess an untapped talent. How exciting it is to discover that you have skills, talents and abilities you never knew you had! For example, many who were initially petrified of public speaking have become our finest speakers. Hundreds of people who thought they were bad at math, after taking a course or investing in private tutoring discover they truly enjoy it. Some who find themselves struggling to make a relationship work, learn patience and become masters at loving unconditionally.

Do you give up because it gets a little difficult? Trust that Universal Wisdom has a purpose. This is indeed the most gratifying aspect of manifesting your heart's desires. You will develop talents and abilities you never knew you had while growing into a more complete person. You will break the chains which have bound you with the belief that you were not enough. The rewards you receive by staying with your heart's desire are not only the accomplishment of your goal, but are literally *self-actualization*.

C HAPTER T WELVE

SUMMARY

"Keep fresh before me the moments of my high resolve."
—Howard Thurman

The manifestation of our true desires is a process. Just as seeds become plants, flowers bloom and winter gives way to spring, the fulfillment of our desires should be a natural and spontaneous process. For most of us, however, this process takes some disciplined effort. The effort involved is not about making it happen, it is about releasing encrusted belief systems that have been obscuring the limitless good which is our natural birthright. It is a process of breaking through our self-imposed shell which encases our true Divine reality. If you have learned anything from this book, it is that as self-expressions of Universal Intelligence we are already beloved, joyous, fulfilled, successful, peaceful, talented, beautiful, prosperous and perfect *now*. It is the entrenched weeds of race mind consciousness, which has us believing otherwise, that must be uprooted. It takes daily discipline to restore the memory of our true essence and to allow the natural process of unfoldment to take place.

This discipline includes taking time each day to do the exercises and processes. Before long, however, these processes will become natural and you will find them *pleasurable*. You'll discover if you skip your daily meditation, affirmation or treatment, you will miss it. This work will become so gratifying that you will look forward to it as a welcome respite from the confusion of this upside-down world. *It will feel like coming home again.* You will begin to see life from a different perspective. As you work with these principles daily, the all-good of Pure Spirit within you will reveal Itself through you. Your purpose will become clear and you will find yourself expressing more of your authentic self. As you become firmly grounded in Spirit, its allness will *automatically* out-picture in your life in seemingly miraculous ways.

One caveat: Once you've learned and have demonstrated these Principles in your life, there may be a temptation to "preach" the Truth to those who you feel need help. Even though you may be thinking it, resist the temptation to say, "If you would only change your consciousness, your life would change!" The first voice that comes back to you will be their ego-voice which, as you know by now, is resistant to change. Better to silently send them love, and then perhaps gently share with them this or other books on spiritual principle. (An order form for additional copies is provided in the back of this book.) Also, after you've been practicing these techniques for a time and have become more peaceful, centered and whole, and after an abundance of good has begun to manifest in your life, others will be more interested in hearing how you did it!

One last time, let's turn to Troward:

"And thus the deepest problems of philosophy bring us back to the old statement of the Law: Ask and ye shall receive, seek and ye shall find, knock and it shall be opened unto you. This is the summing-up of the natural law of the relation between us and the Divine Mind. It is thus no vain boast that Mental Science can enable us to make our lives what we will. We must start from where we are now, and by rightly estimating our relation to the Divine Universal Mind, we can gradually grow into any condition we desire provided we first make ourselves in habitual mental attitude the person who corresponds to those conditions; for we can never get over the law of correspondence, and the externalization will always be in accord with the internal principle that gives rise to it."

The 15-Step Action Plan

Following are 15 specific steps you can use to create that "internal principle" which will facilitate the manifestation of your desires:

1. If you have not yet done so, set your intention for the manifestation of your heart's desires based on the visioning process in Chapter One. Review your Blueprint for Success daily while repeating the accompanying affirmation.

2. Take an occasional day to go out into nature and meditate on the limitless essence and oneness of all creation.

3. Remind yourself who you truly are by repeating the phrase, *"I accept God's will of happiness for me. It is what I am"* as often as possible throughout the day. If it is God's will, it has already been established. You need only acknowledge and accept it.

4. "Be ye transformed by the renewing of your mind." Become *mindful* that the Law of Mind is always responding to your beliefs about yourself by reflecting them back as *form* and *experience* in your life. Take your mind off auto-pilot and listen to your self-talk. If you hear any impossibility thinking, replace it with possibility thinking. The Law will then use this new mold to create limitless possibilities of good in your life.

5. If you are aware of situations that "push your buttons" or that "bring up your stuff" you can re-create your experience by reprogramming your mental computer ahead of time. Refer to the exercise in Chapter Four: *Our Creative Nature*.

6. Continue to observe your behavior to check whether you are in alignment with the false self or your authentic self. Affirm your commitment to expressing your authentic self. The moment self-doubt creeps in, journal your thoughts and feelings until you become clear about who you really are. Then, engage in a positive activity.

7. Make sure you have done all the exercises in Chapter Six: *Core Beliefs*. Do affirmations to correct erroneous core beliefs which have originated either from the false self or from the collective unconscious. Also, *repeat your affirmations throughout the day to keep your consciousness clear.*

8. Create a new thought atmosphere of prosperity, love, success, peace, joy or any good you desire to see increased in your life by visualizing your thought atmosphere filled with an abundance of these qualities. Do this exercise right before falling off to sleep.

9. Clear your consciousness of all resentment. Do the exercises for forgiving others and forgiving yourself. Develop a forgiving attitude by setting your intention to see the authentic self of each and every one you meet.

10. Develop an attitude of gratitude. Give thanks daily for the good in your life. Appreciate the Source of all good. Share your good with others.

11. Meditate daily. Unify with the Divine center within you to experience Its peaceful timelessness. Listen for Its guidance.

12. Every morning upon rising, read a few pages of inspirational material to set your mind thinking in the right direction.

13. Do spiritual mind treatment daily until your specific good is manifest.

14. Spend time in the silence courting your inner wisdom. Start driving with the car radio / tape player *off*. Resist the urge to turn on the television at home to fill up the silence.

15. Move into action following divine guidance.

Your commitment to following the above steps will most assuredly reap bountiful rewards. The following passage by Howard Thurman inspires me to remain centered in my commitment to practice these spiritual principles daily. I hope it does for you as well.

> "In the quietness of this place, surrounded by the all-pervading Presence of God, my heart whispers: Keep fresh before me the moments of my high resolve, that in fair weather or in foul, in good times or in tempests, in the days when the darkness and the foe are nameless or familiar, I may not forget that to which my life is committed."
> —Howard Thurman, *For The Inward Journey*

Limitless love to you on your journey home to the Kingdom you have already inherited!

APPENDIX
RESOURCE GUIDE

The following pages contain a list of recommended reading and resources to support you in continuing this extraordinary adventure of discovering your authentic self, and experiencing more love, joy and fulfillment in your life.

RECOMMENDED READING:

Life and Teaching of the Masters of the Far East by Baird T. Spalding — DeVorss & Co. Publishers (Marina Del Rey, CA): A five volume set about Mr. Spalding's magnificent adventures with several "spiritual masters" in the Himalayas.

The Science of Mind by Ernest Holmes — Science of Mind Publications (Los Angeles): The classic masterpiece explaining how to use New Thought principles to heal your life.

Living the Science of Mind by Ernest Holmes — DeVorss & Company Publishers (Marina Del Rey, CA) An updated and sometimes easier to comprehend version of the original.

A Course In Miracles — Published by The Foundation for Inner Peace (Library of Congress Catalogue Card # 7620363) This is a dense three volume set; a Textbook, a Workbook which has 365 meditations/exercises to do, one each day for a year, and the Guide for Teachers. This course takes real commitment, but it will transform your life.

Autobiography of a Yogi by Paramahansa Yogananda — Published by Self-Realization Fellowship (Los Angeles, CA) Yogananda's personal transformation from student to Yogi(Master). Inspirational accounts of Cosmic Consciousness achieved through meditation.

A Return to Love by Marianne Williamson — Harper Collins Publishers. Ms. Williamson's down to earth interpretation of A Course In Miracles. This was a best-seller for many months. Powerful.

Ageless Body, Timeless Mind by Deepak Chopra, MD — Harmony Books (New York). A scientific explanation of spiritual/mind/body concepts. Mind-expanding. Also wonderful is *Creating Affluence* by Dr. Chopra. Timeless wisdom for becoming more prosperous.

SuperBeings, Practical Spirituality and *Planetary Commission* (includes a workbook) by John Randolph Price — The Quartus Foundation for Spiritual Research (Austin, Texas). These books will clear away the clouds in your consciousness to allow the light of Truth to shine.

Love is the Answer by Gerald G. Jampolsky, MD, and Diane Cirincione — Bantam Books (New York) A wonderful guide to creating positive relationships. Includes dozens of humorous, yet revealing illustrations.

Spiritual Economics by Eric Butterworth — Unity School of Christianity (Unity Village, Missouri). The Spiritual principles behind the Law of Abundance. Profound wisdom, yet easy to understand.

Scientific Christian Mental Practice by Emma Curtis Hopkins — DeVorss & Company Publishers. A true mystic, Ms. Hopkins shares some amazing insights in this book. The language is a little old and she emphasizes the "Christian" element. If that doesn't bother you, you'll find it a true inspiration.

The Edinburgh & Dore Lectures on Mental Science by Thomas Troward — DeVorss & Co. Publishers. If you like absolute Truth and direct inspiration, this is the book for you! Troward's only flaws are very long sentences and paragraphs that go on for pages. However, his insights were truly genius.

Emerson's Essays by Ralph Waldo Emerson — Harper & Row Perennial Library. This is timeless inspiration.

Journey of Awakening by Ram Dass, Bantam Books — Explains the purpose and benefits of meditation as well as giving the reader dozens of meditation styles. Includes a resource guide. One caveat: the philosophy in this book is fundamentally Eastern, which generally promotes the elimination of desire.

The Blooming of a Lotus by Thich Nhat Hanh — Parallax Press, Berkeley, California. Excellent guided meditations.

Pathway of Roses by Christian D. Larson — Newcastle Publishing, Van Nuys, California. Beautifully written, poetic, timeless spiritual Truth.

Spirits In Rebellion by Charles S. Braden — Southern Methodist University Press, Dallas. The story of the beginning and growth of the New Thought and kindred American Metaphysical Movements.

Homesick For Heaven by Walter Starcke — Guadalupe Press, Boerne, Texas. He closes the gap between living a spiritual life and a successful, creative life in the world.

Practicing The Presence by Joel Goldsmith — HarperCollins Publishers, New York. One of America's greatest Christian mystics. Inspirational, Absolute Truth.

RESOURCES:

Transcendental Meditation Society 1-800-608-8602 Meditation instruction, group meditation and lectures. They can refer you to a TM center in your city.

Self-Realization Fellowship 213-225-2471 Meditation instruction, classes and services. This is their worldwide Headquarters. Again, they can refer you to a local group.

Science of Mind Magazine (published by a division of United Church of Religious Science) 213-388-2181 — 3251 W. 6th Street. P.O. Box 75127 Los Angeles, CA 90075. This monthly magazine is jam packed with daily meditations, affirmations, and articles by people who have demonstrated Truth in their lives. Includes interviews with leaders in the New Thought field.

Religious Science Church or Science of Mind Center To find one in your area, call: (213) 388-2181. Or write: Science of Mind, 3251 West Sixth Street, Los Angeles, CA 90020. A list of centers in the United States and internationally is also listed in the back of the Science of Mind magazine. You can also reach them on-line: http://www.scienceofmind.com

Metaphysical Bookstores In every major city there is at least one Metaphysical Bookstore. Go there and browse the shelves and check out their bulletin board. You will find meditation classes and groups that meet to discuss ideas based on Truth. Shop around to find something that feels right to you.

The Quartus Foundation Located in Texas. They have a superb monthly newsletter, The Quartus Report. You may contact them at 210-537-4689, or write them at P.O. Box 1768, Boerne, TX 78006-6768.

Institute of Noetic Sciences Located in Sausalito, California. They have an excellent quarterly review and bulletin dedicated to the development of human consciousness through scientific inquiry, spirtual understanding and psychological well-being. 800-383-1394.

World Ministry of Prayer A 24-hour prayer hotline personed by dedicated professionals who are there to prayer with you. Prayer hotline number: 213-385-0209

Agape Prayer Ministry Another 24-hour prayer hotline provided by dedicated professionals: 310-453-6638

To order the *MANIFESTING YOUR DESIRES: GUIDED EXERCISES AND PROCESSES* audio-cassette use the order form below. To order additional copies of the book, use order form on the reverse page, Please fill out completely and send along with your check or money order to:

SELF-MASTERY PRESS
P.O. Box 57272
Sherman Oaks, CA 91413

Or, call toll free 24 hours a day:
1-800-637-2256

We will send *MANIFESTING YOUR DESIRES* immediately to you, or to the person you specify.

From Self-Mastery Press: "MANIFESTING YOUR DESIRES: GUIDED EXERCISES AND PROCESSES"

Please send ____ audiocassettes of *Manifesting Your Desires: Guided Exercises and Processes* to the following:

Name: _____

Address:_____

City, State:_____

Zip: _____

Each: $10.95
Postage &
  Handling $ 2.00
Total: $12.95

CA residents add $0.90 tax

Enclosed is my check or money order for $_____

From Self-Mastery Press: "MANIFESTING YOUR DESIRES: HOW TO APPLY TIMELESS SPIRITUAL TRUTHS TO ACHIEVE FULFILLMENT"

Please send _____ copies of the book, *Manifesting Your Desires* to the following:

Name: _____

Address:_____

City, State:_____

Zip: _____

Each: $19.95
Postage &
Handling $ 3.50
Total: $23.45

CA residents add $1.65 tax

Enclosed is my check or money order for $_____